John T. Wilder

UNION GENERAL, SOUTHERN INDUSTRIALIST

MERCER UNIVERSITY

MERCER UNIVERSITY PRESS

Endowed by

TOM WATSON BROWN

and

THE WATSON-BROWN FOUNDATION, INC.

John T. Wilder

UNION GENERAL, SOUTHERN INDUSTRIALIST

Steven Cox

MERCER UNIVERSITY PRESS
Macon, Georgia

MUP/ H1032

Published by Mercer University Press
1501 Mercer University Drive
Macon, Georgia 31207

27 26 25 24 23 5 4 3 2 1

Books published by Mercer University Press are printed on acid-free paper that meets the requirements of the American National Standard for Information Sciences—Permanence of Paper for Printed Library Materials.

Printed and bound in the United States.

This book is set in Adobe Garamond.

Cover/jacket design by Burt&Burt.

ISBN 978-0-88146-884-7
Cataloging-in-Publication Data is available from the Library of Congress

Contents

Preface

John Thomas Wilder (1830–1917) led a full, productive, and resourceful life. He is primarily remembered today by Civil War scholars and enthusiasts in what can almost be seen as a cult following. His achievements and service as an Indiana Union Army officer during the Civil War are certainly noteworthy, as he displayed some important—and occasionally unorthodox—traits of leadership and command, often to impressive effect. His prewar and postwar years, however, have received little notice. The only existing full biographical treatment of Wilder, titled *General John T. Wilder*, was published in 1936, just nineteen years after Wilder's death in 1917. It was written by Samuel Cole Williams (1864–1947), Tennessee historian and one-time member of the Tennessee Supreme Court, and published by Indiana University Press. Williams, who wrote just over a dozen histories from 1924 to 1947, mostly related to Tennessee, wrote the Wilder biography in the middle of his canon of work. It is a short biography of fifty pages but appendices add bulk to the book. Of the fifty pages devoted to Wilder's life, forty-two deal with Wilder's experiences and achievements during the Civil War. Williams's biography contains some errors or exaggerations, and other claims are not particularly well documented. That it was published by an Indiana academic press is no surprise. Indiana takes great pride in Wilder, who lived in the state in the 1850s and early 1860s and, during the Civil War, commanded the Indiana 17th Infantry Regiment—despite the fact that he permanently left Indiana shortly after the war ended. It is quite possible Samuel Cole Williams personally knew Wilder in his later years, as both lived in Johnson City, Tennessee, during the same period.

It is not my intention to debunk previous accounts, but discrepancies with Williams's account of Wilder's life are briefly discussed in the notes.

Prior to Williams's book, biographical information on Wilder was scarce. The first biographical treatment was likely the few pages devoted to Wilder found in the *Annals of the Army of the Cumberland*, compiled by John Fitch and first published in 1863 by J. B. Lippincott (Philadelphia). The *Annals* had a section devoted to short biographies of key officers, including Wilder. One may assume the source of information on Wilder came from Wilder himself, who was making a name for himself in the Union Army despite being only thirty-three years old at the time. Subsequent points found in later biographical treatments, including Williams's biography, seem to rely heavily on this 1863 account.

Information detailing Wilder's prewar years, particularly that of his early industrial work, is sparse. What is known is that in the early 1850s Wilder made his way from his boyhood home in the Catskill Mountains in New York to Columbus, Ohio, for an apprenticeship in a foundry. After the apprenticeship, he moved to Indiana to start his own foundry. Accounts vary as to where in Indiana he first settled, and when, but it appears he began his millwork in either Lawrenceburg or Greensburg, possibly as early as 1852. He had mills in both towns in the 1850s, and, when the Civil War broke out in 1861, he had a successful mill in Greensburg. The brief biography in the *Annals* mentions that Wilder was a much-consulted specialist in the field of hydraulics in a number of states prior to the war. Given his various patents on hydraulic works, both before and after the war, this claim is credible. The libraries and historical societies in both towns are certainly aware of Wilder's history with their towns but unfortunately have very little information concerning his industrial works there. The Indiana State Library and Archives in Indianapolis has a sizeable collection of Wilder correspondence, some wartime, others postwar.

Many Civil War scholars are aware of, if not fascinated by, Wilder's war years and his "Lightning Brigade." However, this biography should not be treated merely as a Civil War history. Like Williams's biography, the war does take up a large portion of this work, even though Wilder was most active in it only from 1861 until the Battle of Chickamauga in summer 1863 and then again briefly in 1864. Researchers primarily interested in Wilder's war years and accomplishments should consult Richard Baumgartner's *Blue Lightning: Wilder's Mounted Infantry Brigade in the Battle of Chickamauga* (Blue Acorn Press, 1997) or Glenn Sunderland's *Lightning at Hoover's Gap* (T. Yosellof, 1969, later reissued as *Wilder's Lightning Brigade—and Its Spencer Repeaters*). There are also many articles relating to Wilder and his Lighting Brigade in periodicals devoted to the Civil War and history.

Wilder's contribution to industry, particularly in the South during Reconstruction, has been overlooked. He was an entrepreneur and often had several projects and business interests either overlapping briefly or operating at the same time. He developed mines and foundries but also built hotels, started a railroad company, offered his services to the government and military, and even got involved in politics. He moved to and maintained a permanent home in Chattanooga, Tennessee, in 1866, but in the following decades also had homes in various towns in east Tennessee, as he continuously started up businesses and enterprises throughout the eastern part of the state. He is associated with several projects, such as the establishment of Chattanooga University in 1886 (now the University of

Tennessee at Chattanooga) and the development of the Chickamauga Civil War Battlefield as the first national military park. Records show that his involvement in the university and military park seems to have been limited, relying mostly on the use of his name as an endorsement.

Wilder led a colorful, active life. His 1904 marriage to a much younger woman ten years after the death of his first wife brings to mind the 1989 award-winning novel by Alan Gurganus, *The Oldest Living Confederate Widow Tells All.* Though fiction, Gurganus's book was based on documented occasions of aging soldiers from both sides of the war marrying much younger women. These wives often would outlive their husbands by several decades; some wives were quite young when they married elderly veterans, so a few widows lived well into the second half of the twentieth century.

Even in his last years, John T. Wilder was quite involved with travel and business. He was well respected by veterans on both sides of the war and idolized by the men he commanded. His legacy has not been forgotten, and his name is still mentioned in the places he inhabited more than a century ago.

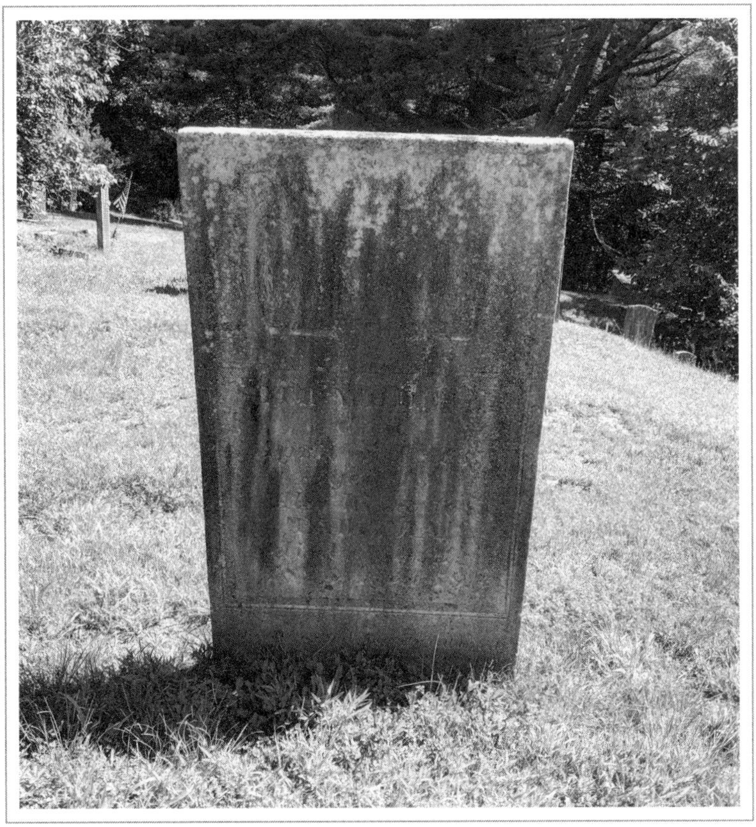

Grave of Seth Wilder, grandfather of John T. Wilder,
in West Cummington, Massachusetts.

Courtesy Steven Cox

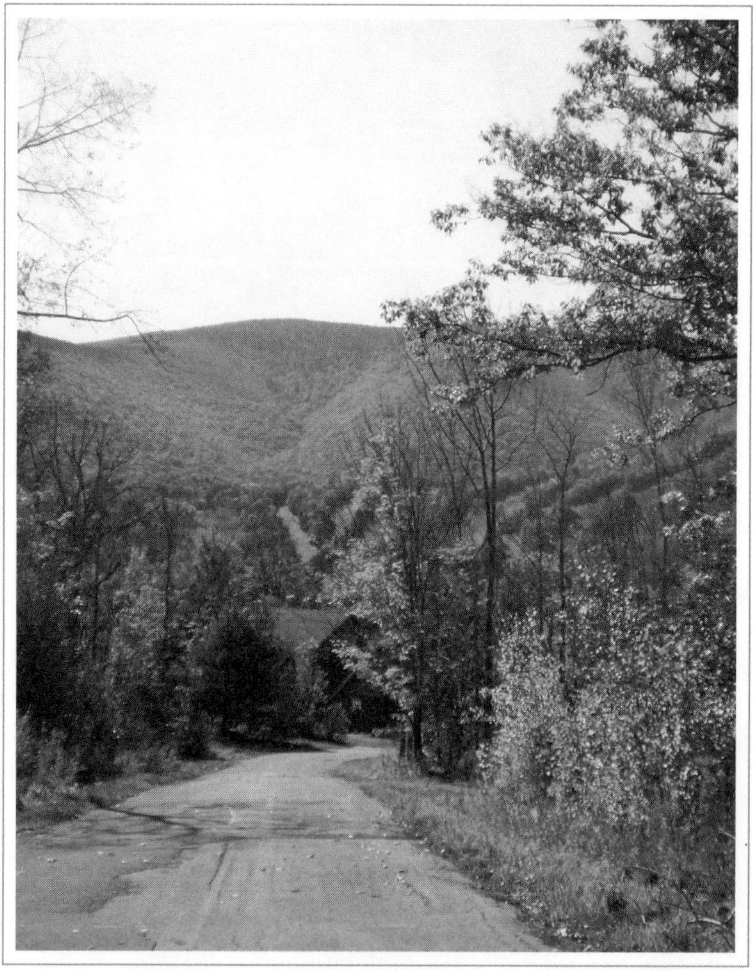

Road leading in to Hunter, New York,
birthplace of John T. Wilder, present day.

Courtesy Steven Cox

John T. Wilder, ca. 1860s.

Photo from *Indiana at Chickamauga, 1863–1900: Report of Indiana Commissioners Chickamauga National Military Park, Indianapolis* (1901)

John T. Wilder, ca. 1860s.

Courtesy Becky Everett

John T. Wilder at the Cloudland Hotel, ca. 1880s.

Courtesy Becky Everett

John T. Wilder in his 60s, ca. 1890s.

Courtesy Becky Everett

Colonel Milo Hascall, commander of the Indiana 17th Infantry, and Wilder's first commanding officer.

Photo from *Photographic History of the Civil War* (1911)

Colonel Joseph J. Reynolds, of the 10th Indiana Volunteers, who commanded Union troops in West Virginia.

Photo from *Photographic History of the Civil War* (1911)

General William Rosecrans,
commander of the Army of the Cumberland.

Photo from *Photographic History of the Civil War* (1911)

General Braxton Bragg,
commander of the Confederate Army of Tennessee.

Photo from *Photographic History of the Civil War* (1911)

General Simon Bolivar Buckner, Confederate officer who Wilder appealed to at Munfordville, Kentucky, before surrender.

Photo from *Photographic History of the Civil War* (1911)

General George H. Thomas, Union officer in the Army of the Cumberland who Wilder supported during the Battle of Chickamauga.

Photo from *Photographic History of the Civil War* (1911)

Hiram S. Chamberlain (1835–1916),
Wilder's partner with the Roane Iron Company.

Roane Iron Company, Rockwood, Tennessee.

Courtesy Roane County Heritage Commission

The Cloudland Hotel, atop Roan Mountain
in eastern Tennessee and western North Carolina.

Courtesy Archives of Appalachia, East Tennessee State University, Johnson City, Tennessee

Foundation of the Cloudland Hotel
on Roan Mountain, present day.

Courtesy Steven Cox

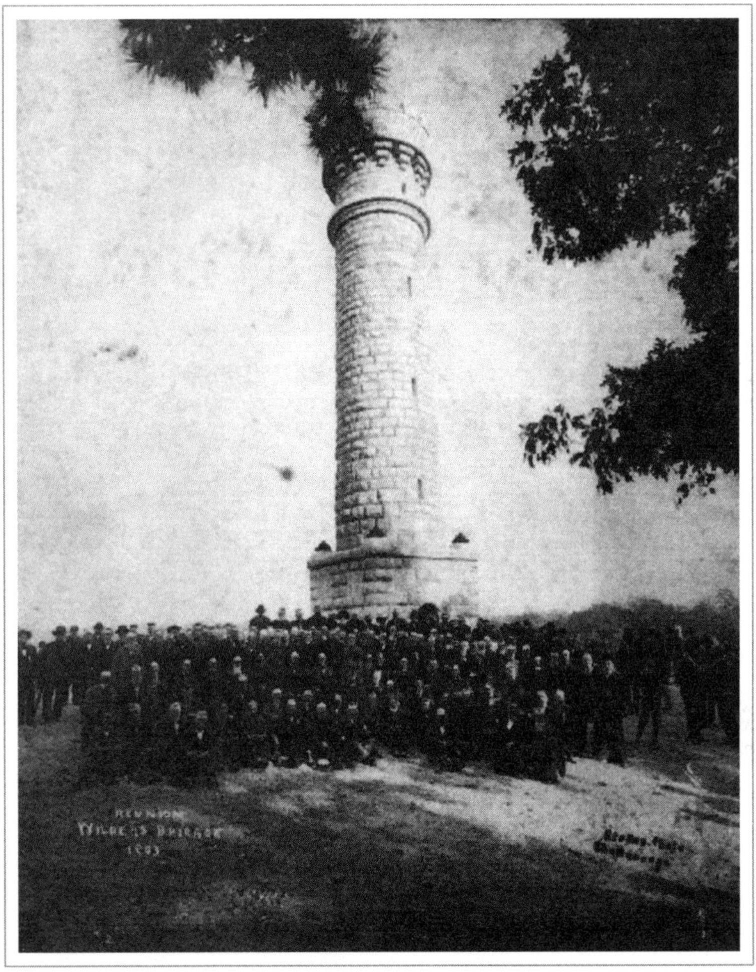

Lightning Brigade Reunion, Chickamauga-Chattanooga Military National Park, shortly after completion of the Wilder Tower, 1893.

Courtesy Becky Everett

The Wilder Tower at the Chickamauga-Chattanooga Military National Park, present day.

Courtesy Steven Cox

Dora Lee Wilder, John T. Wilder's second (and much younger) wife, ca. 1890s.

Courtesy Special Collections at Tennessee Tech University, Cookeville, Tennessee

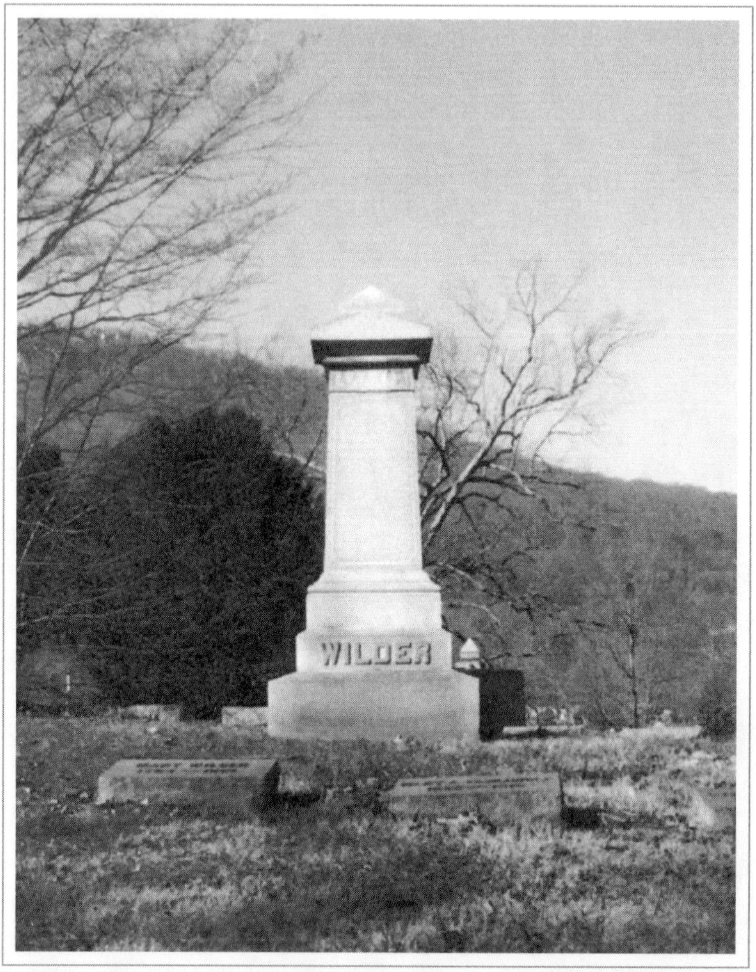

Wilder Family Plot, Forest Hills Cemetery in St. Elmo, Tennessee, with Lookout Mountain looming in the background.

Courtesy Steven Cox

John T. Wilder

UNION GENERAL, SOUTHERN INDUSTRIALIST

Introduction

During the first decades following the American Civil War, a period known as the Reconstruction Era in the South, Chattanooga, Tennessee, became the home of many former Union officers and soldiers. The city's industrial resources attracted Northern and Midwestern industrialists, bankers, and businessmen. Because key battles had been fought nearby, many had been in the area during the war. In September 1863, Union and Confederate forces fought south of Chattanooga in the bloody battle at Chickamauga in north Georgia. This battle would be one of the Confederacy's last major victories. As a result, Union forces retreated into Chattanooga where they were besieged by the victorious Rebels. Two months later, Union forces rallied in Chattanooga and broke the siege at the Battle of Missionary Ridge and the Battle of Lookout Mountain (known as the "Battle above the Clouds"). Chattanooga remained in Union control for the remainder of the war.

Many of the Union veterans who returned to Chattanooga after the war were not the traditional carpetbaggers, but enterprising individuals who would become the city's leading citizens. Chattanooga (and most of eastern Tennessee) had been pro-Union throughout the war, so the Union veterans were readily accepted into the city. Even Confederate veterans seemed willing to put the war differences aside and come to a comfortable, if not friendly, alliance with them. It was, in a way, a second invasion of the city by Yankees; the first had been in summer 1863 when Union troops attacked the city, firing from nearby Stringer's Ridge and Cameron Hill. These Union soldiers and officers included future pharmaceutical pioneer Eli Lilly and industrialist, inventor, and entrepreneur John T. Wilder, of Greensburg, Indiana, commander of the 17th Indiana

Infantry. Many Chattanooga citizens had already fled the city, in anticipation of the invasion. As cannonballs rained down on the city from the nearby hills, churchgoers attending a service felt the brunt of the attack, as a cannonball took the steeple off the church. The pastor was in mid-prayer, and many of the congregation quietly slipped out to seek a safer sanctuary while the preacher, unfazed by the attack, continued his prayer. Newspaperman Henry Watterson, one of the editors of the *Chattanooga Rebel*, decided he would remain in the church until the end of the prayer, which turned out to be, as he put it, "the longest prayer I ever heard."[1]

Four years is but a small portion of a full lifetime, but in acquitting himself favorably in a major event such as the American Civil War, John T. Wilder became forever linked and associated with that period, apart from his later achievements. While growing up in the Catskill Mountains of New York, Wilder may not have aspired to serving in the military and being a soldier or officer. As a young student, he was inclined toward geology, which directed him to a career in mining and industry. That he distinguished himself militarily might not be a surprise, however, as he was descended from ancestors who gave good accounts of themselves in the Revolutionary War and the War of 1812.

After the Civil War, many Union officers and soldiers returned to Chattanooga, attracted by the milder climate and the possibilities that the region offered. The city even solicited Northern businessmen, industrialists, and bankers to move there. As a result, Chattanooga grew in the decades leading into the twentieth century. Many of the Northerners, who now identified first and foremost as Chattanoogans, rather than Yankees, prospered in politics as well as business and became

[1] Watterson, *"Marse Henry,"* 309.

leading citizens of the city they helped develop. By the early 1900s, Civil War veterans all over the country were dying each day by the hundreds, if not thousands, including these Chattanooga citizens. But they had done their good work, and with their good work, Chattanooga became known as the "Dynamo of Dixie." According to the 1910 census, which registered Civil War service for the first time, only a third of the soldiers who fought for the Union were still living.[2] More than thirty thousand Union veterans were living in federal and state soldiers' homes and collecting pensions. By 1920, the percentage of Civil War veterans still living had dropped to 15 percent.[3] The decline continued through the first half of the twentieth century, and the very last recognized soldiers of the war from either side survived into but not past the 1950s.

One morning in October 1917, death claimed a truly innovative officer and soldier, General John Thomas Wilder. "Death Claims Famous Soldier and Good Citizen" read the *Chattanooga News* front-page obituary for the Union officer who had made Chattanooga his home after the war. "Death Calls General Wilder," read the headline of its rival, the *Chattanooga Sunday Times.* This headline about a Civil War officer shared front-page space with articles about another war in which America would soon be involved and which would later be called World War I. Wilder, who had been long associated with Chattanooga and who had been given the brevet rank of brigadier general in 1864 after his field service ended, had died while visiting Jacksonville, Florida. He was eighty-seven years old. Before the war, he had been successful as a young industrialist with a growing foundry (and family) in Indiana. He had distinguished himself during the war; after enlisting

[2] Logue, *To Appomattox and Beyond*, 131.
[3] Ibid., 135, 137.

enthusiastically and being promoted several times, he brought several innovative and creative methods to leadership and warfare. After the war, he resumed his industrial career and, like other Union soldiers and officers, answered the call to come to Chattanooga, where he set up a home base and developed mines and foundries in the Appalachian region of eastern Tennessee. A businessman, industrialist, civic leader, and briefly a politician, he was a colorful character and seemed to have held close to the maxim "necessity is the mother of invention." He developed industry around the city, the state, and the South and in the process became one of the South's leading industrialists of the nineteenth century. A major monument at the battlefield at Chickamauga bears his name, as does an area on Signal Mountain near Chattanooga, as well as a small town in north central Tennessee. He held patents for hydraulic works that he used in his mines. He traveled during the postwar years to England and Europe and counted many influential citizens as close friends.

Despite being a Northerner, Wilder was well respected and admired in the South, even among Confederate veterans. In Chattanooga it was no different. His influence in that city was remarkable, and he is still remembered today.

Chapter 1

Ancestry and Early Life

Around the year 1850, a young John Thomas Wilder arrived in Columbus, Ohio. He was twenty years of age and looking to advance a career he had begun in the Catskill Mountains of New York, where he had been born. A story that appeared in the *Columbus Journal* shortly after his death related how Wilder, just having arrived in Columbus, found a coin on the ground and picked it up to use for a meal. After arriving at the restaurant, he then decided to wait until a time when he was even hungrier or needier to spend it. Wilder carried that coin in his pocket the rest of his life, according to the article, to prove to himself that he was never completely destitute. If true, the story shows that frugality, discipline, and steadfastness were instilled in him at a young age; these qualities would last through his life as an industrialist, military officer, businessman, and entrepreneur. This same discipline would grow into an astute though sometimes unorthodox resourcefulness. In 1862, this resourcefulness would save not only his life but also the lives of hundreds of soldiers under his command when they faced extermination by an overwhelming Confederate army surrounding Wilder and his troops in Kentucky. John T. Wilder found ways to beat adversity and would be successful with many of his ventures, despite an occasional setback. Coming from strong English stock, Wilder was several generations removed from his ancestors who first came to America. The first generations of American Wilders accustomed themselves to their new country, and when the time came to take up arms against England, they stood by their new home and fought alongside their neighbors for independence. They joined in when and where they were needed. John T. Wilder would do the same.

John T. Wilder's English ancestors first came to America in 1638 and had documented roots in England reaching back to the reign of King Henry VII (the father of the better-known first Tudor king, Henry VIII), who reigned from 1485 to 1509. In 1497, a man named Nicholas Wilder, who preceded John T. Wilder by eight generations and may have been of French or German ancestry, received from King Henry VII an estate named Nunhide in the southern-central region of West Berkshire in England, at the town of Sulham.[1] Nicholas Wilder, who served militarily under Henry VII when Henry was then the Earl of Richmond, had taken part in the defeat of King Richard III at the Battle of Bosworth in 1485. Nicholas remained in the service of Henry VII and in 1497 was awarded the estate in Sulham for his service to the king. This began the homestead of many generations of Wilders, lasting until the late 1700s.

Nicholas Wilder had a son, John, who had a son also named John, and both in turn would inherit the Sulham estate through an entail, a lineal inheritance system popular in England. However, the family also had a home twelve miles away at Shiplake. John, the grandson of Nicholas, married and had seven children—four boys and three girls. One of the four boys, Thomas Wilder, married a woman named Martha (last name unknown), and they had at least two children, Edward and Mary. Religious persecution by King Charles I (who reigned from 1629 until his execution in 1649) was rampant, and many fled to the New World from England. Thomas died in 1634, and in 1638, Martha, Mary, and Edward immigrated

---

[1] Variant spellings of the family name are found from documents from the era, with spellings of *Wylder* and *Wyldar* used.

to the New World aboard the ship *Confidence*, settling in Hingham, Massachusetts. Hingham, south of Boston, was settled in 1633 by White settlers and incorporated in 1635. It took its name from an English village in the county of Norfolk, where its original settlers originated. Hingham remained in the hands of the Wampanoag tribe until 1655, when a formal purchase was arranged. The year before the Wilder family arrived, an Englishman by the name of Samuel Lincoln arrived and settled there. Lincoln was the great-great-great-great grandfather of Abraham Lincoln, and the Lincoln ancestor who first immigrated to North America from England.

It is believed most Wilders today in the United States are descended from Martha, Mary, and Edward.[2] Edward's birth year is estimated around 1623 or 1624 in England, on account of his being made a freeman in America in 1645, which normally happened when one reached the age of twenty-one. As an adult, Edward acquired land, married, and had eleven children, including John, who was born in 1653. For more than one hundred years, Wilders lived in the region of Plymouth and Norfolk Counties of Massachusetts, along the east coast of the state. Edward lived until 1690. His son John lived until 1724, and he and his wife, Rebecca, had seven children, including Ephraim, born in 1696. Ephraim, a blacksmith, married Mary Loring in 1723, and they had nine children, including Seth Wilder, John Thomas Wilder's great-grandfather. By this time, the Wilders had settled a bit south at Abingdon, Massachusetts.

As hostilities between the colonies and Great Britain grew, the Massachusetts Provincial Congress arranged for the creation of companies of soldiers, the famed "Minutemen," and

---

[2] Famous American playwright Thornton Wilder (1897–1975) is also descended from Edward Wilder.

procured the supplies and weapons to equip them. Being a member of a local militia was viewed as a civic obligation at the time. It is with Seth Wilder (1739–1814) that we first see Wilders acquitting themselves favorably in war in North America, as Seth served in the militia and is believed to have fought and lost a leg in the Battle of Bunker Hill at Boston in summer 1775. He was one of more than three hundred colonists injured during the fight, which resulted in high casualties suffered by the British, who were victorious nonetheless. He may have even been previously involved with the Boston Tea Party in late 1773; an 1858 newspaper article from the *Lowell (MA) Daily Citizen and News* refers to a Seth Wilder of Hingham having participated in the "throwing overboard the tea in Boston Harbor."[3] His son Seth Wilder Jr. (1763–1814), at the age of sixteen, would take his father's place in the militia. In July 1779, he was injured by a bayonet during the Battle of Stony Point, approximately thirty miles north of today's New York City. Colonialists, under General "Mad" Anthony Wayne, outnumbered the British Army under command of General Henry Johnson and won that battle, capturing British supplies and arms and boosting morale among the colonists.

Seth Wilder Jr. survived his wound and the Revolutionary War. He would marry Tabitha Dorcas Briggs, most likely in Cummington, Massachusetts, slightly east of the Berkshire Mountains of western Massachusetts. Cummington was a small village, first settled in 1762 and incorporated in 1779. Poet and newspaper editor William Cullen Bryant would be born there in 1794. Tabitha Dorcas Briggs's ancestry is not known, but she may have been related to James Briggs, Cummington's Congregational Church minister. She was also possibly related to a future governor of Massachusetts (1831–

[3] *Lowell (MA) Daily Citizen and News*, 22 January 1858.

1833), George Nixon Briggs. Seth and Tabitha Wilder would have three children: Reuben, William, and Townsend. Working as a mechanic before, during, and after the war, Seth would die shortly before his father, Seth Sr., in 1814. Both were buried in the small village of West Cummington.

Reuben Wilder (1793–1873), the father of John Thomas Wilder, was born and raised in Cummington and had played with William Cullen Bryant as a child. Reuben answered the call of his father and grandfather (and his ancestor, Nicholas) and also served his country during the War of 1812. In 1813, he participated in the Battle of Sacket's Harbor (on the eastern coast of Lake Ontario in New York), an American victory, and in 1814 in the Battle of Plattsburgh (northeast New York and also known as the Battle of Lake Champlain), also an American victory. At some point after the war, Reuben settled in Hunter's Village (Hunter today) in the Catskill Mountains of New York. It was there, in 1825, that he married Mary Merritt (1793–1876), a native of Hunter's Village. They had five children—two sons and three daughters. One of those two sons was John Thomas Wilder.[4]

John Thomas Wilder was born on 31 January 1830, the first-born child of Reuben and Mary Wilder. His boyhood and early school years were spent in the Catskill Mountains, in Hunter's Village, a fledgling village in Greene County. This was the land of Washington Irving and the locale of his story "Rip Van Winkle." Sparsely settled in the early 1800s, the region had been the site of a land grant in the early 1700s from Queen Anne to Johannes Hardenbergh, an early settler in the area. Very little clearing was done with this heavily and densely forested land. Even the Indians of the area found little use for

---

[4] Most of the information concerning Wilder's ancestors can be found in Moses Wilder, *The Book of the Wilders* (New York: E. O. Jenkins, 1878).

it, leaving it for the wild animals that lived there.[5] The land grant was later contested, and the twenty-thousand-acre property was subsequently divided and given to several individuals in 1780. One of the men who received land was John Hunter, and the village was named for him. Some of the subsequent settlers may have been Tories, run out of nearby Putnam County, while others were lumbermen from Connecticut. Crude roads were set in the dense countryside, and in 1813 Hunter's Village was formed out of a nearby hamlet called Windham. The town is surrounded by mountains in the Catskill range, with Hunter Mountain (today a ski resort) towering over the town. Tanneries were set up, giving the name to a nearby town, Tannersville. Wilder's school days in the 1830s and 40s were spent in Hunter's Village, a growing town that already had several school districts by the time he started school. By the 1840s, there were already more than a hundred small schools throughout Greene County. There is little doubt Wilder received a good education as early county histories make note that the schoolmasters were known to be strict disciplinarians. A school term lasted seven months, and even though the area was rural and remote, students and teachers had access to the standard schoolbooks available at that time. For leisure activities, the village had spelling bees, singing events, and lively debates. The main industry in Hunter's Village was furniture.

The earliest biographical sketch of John T. Wilder, found in the Civil War-era *Annals of the Army of the Cumberland* (mentioned in the introduction), has a four-and-a-half-page biographical narrative of Wilder, who was then an officer in the Union Army during the Civil War. He was only thirty-three years of age at the time of this publication. The source for this

[5] Wiltse, *Pioneer Days in the Catskill High Peaks*, 17–18.

biography cannot be determined, but one may assume it was Wilder himself. The first sentence in the *Annals* differs from later accounts of Wilder's birth, claiming Wilder was born in Ulster County, New York. In the 1850 census, the Wilder family, along with John, is listed for the town of Olive, in Ulster County, approximately thirty miles south of Hunter's Village. Reuben, Wilder's father, is listed as a millwright, as is the twenty-year-old John. Some accounts of Wilder have him leaving New York when he was still in his late teens, but if the census is correct, he still would have been in New York in 1850 when he was twenty. Later, Samuel Cole Williams would include in his 1936 biography of Wilder some information concerning Wilder's ancestors that is first found in the *Annals*. In the 1860 census, Reuben Wilder, still listed as living in Olive, is entered as a "master millwright." By this time, his son John had already left New York and was making a name for himself further west.

According to biographer Samuel Cole Williams, Wilder left New York for the Midwest at the age of nineteen, which would have been some time in 1849 or January 1850. Although the exact date Wilder left New York is not known, it is evident that he did leave New York for Ohio during this period.

As White settlement increased and populations grew, mining operations and foundries had seen expansion west in the 1840s and were beginning to equal, if not outnumber, those found along the East Coast and New England. The development of the railroad and rail lines allowed the transportation of supplies into Ohio, Illinois, and Indiana. It was not far from Pittsburgh, Pennsylvania, where foundries were numerous, to Ohio, and the young John Wilder evidently aimed to get in on this industrial expansion.

Wilder, a young man with little money in his pockets, traveled to Columbus, Ohio, and found work at a foundry run by a Mr. Joseph Ridgway.[6] Why Wilder chose Columbus is not known, but it is possible he previously secured an apprenticeship with Ridgway. Joseph Ridgway, a New Yorker himself, had started his Columbus foundry in 1822, the first in the area. Ridgway was also a politician and served from 1837 to 1843 in the Ohio Congress. His foundry, the Ridgway Iron Foundry, manufactured plows, first by horsepower and later by steam, and was one of the earliest successful manufacturing companies in Columbus. By the late 1840s, Ridgway's foundry employed more than fifty workers.[7] After bringing a nephew into the business, Ridgway began producing other machinery such as steam engines and stoves. By the time Wilder began working, they also ran a railway car factory.[8] According to Williams, Wilder worked as a millwright, draftsman, and pattern maker.[9] Since the 1850 census listed Wilder as a millwright in Olive, New York, Wilder apparently had experience before joining Ridgway in Ohio. Wilder must have been a quick study and learned more of the trade working for Ridgway, certainly enough to branch out while still in his twenties to start a foundry of his own.

Accounts vary as to when Wilder left Columbus and the Ridgway Iron Foundry, but Williams claims Wilder excelled at the foundry to the point that Ridgway offered him partnership in the business. Wilder had grown professionally and was reportedly regarded as an expert in the field of hydraulics. Where Wilder landed next is uncertain, as varying accounts place him

---

[6] Williams, *Wilder*, 2.

[7] Lee, *History of the City of Columbus*, 2:318–19.

[8] Taylor, *Centennial History*, 332, 334.

[9] Williams, *Wilder*, 2.

in two southern Indiana towns in the early 1850s. Many accounts have Wilder arriving at Greensburg, Indiana (Decatur County), in 1857 or 1858, but other accounts have him first starting an enterprise in Lawrenceburg, Indiana (Dearborn County), on the Ohio River, around 1852. Lawrenceburg is approximately twenty-five miles west of Cincinnati and approximately thirty-five miles from Greensburg. Both Lawrenceburg and Greensburg are more than one hundred miles west of Columbus, so Wilder set up his foundry quite a distance from Ridgway. One bit of evidence that he had business interests in Lawrenceburg comes from a story in a 1936 *Chattanooga Times* article, which mentions Wilder had a partnership with a Lawrenceburg banker named William Probasco. Their enterprise received an offer to purchase a whiskey distillery, and Wilder, a lifelong teetotaler, ended the partnership when Probasco was in favor of buying it.[10] The Probasco family would eventually end up in Chattanooga, Tennessee, as would Wilder. Wilder's association with the town of Lawrenceburg continued after he moved to Greensburg later in the 1850s. Newspaper articles from the 1880s report Wilder's wife, Martha, visiting friends in Lawrenceburg, and his daughter visiting an aunt there as well. Martha, whom Wilder married in 1858, was from Greensburg but may have had a sister in Lawrenceburg.

An undated article, circa 1925 in the *Greensburg Daily News*, reports Wilder coming to Greensburg around 1851 or 1852. Other accounts placed Wilder in Lawrenceburg as late as 1859, and it's possible Wilder had homes and foundries simultaneously in both Lawrenceburg and Greensburg throughout the 1850s. After the Civil War, as he settled back into the business of industry, he would have homes and foundries in various

[10] T. A. Rogers, *Chattanooga Times*, 20 December 1936.

parts of Tennessee while maintaining a permanent home in Chattanooga.

Indiana achieved statehood in late 1816. By early 1850, Indiana was largely agricultural and had the seventh-largest population (of the thirty-one states) in the United States. However, most Indiana cities, including Indianapolis, had fewer than eight thousand people. Industry was beginning to develop as outsiders moved in to take advantage of its railways and resources.[11] Governor Joseph A. Wright, who previously championed agriculture, called for the development of industry and manufacturing statewide in 1853. The presence of coal in the southern part of Indiana was already known, and in the mid-1830s the American Cannel Coal Company had been founded in Perry County, in south Indiana. Coal production increased in the early 1850s, primarily due to a railroad opening up connecting Terra Haute to Indianapolis.[12]

Lawrenceburg, Indiana, in the 1850s had a population of approximately twenty-five hundred people. Several flour mills, furniture and cigar factories, woolen mills, stove foundries, and other mills and enterprises were fortified by two railroads coming into town, the Ohio and Mississippi and the Lawrenceburg and Indianapolis. The town would have been attractive to Wilder to start a foundry, with the trains, the river, and the region. Wilder did register at least one patent, for a portable grist mill, during his years in Lawrenceburg. But the town did not grow, despite the two railway lines, and this stagnation may have been a reason Wilder eventually left Lawrenceburg.

In the 1850s, as a young foundry owner and businessman, Wilder developed professional and personal relationships with Indiana bankers, businessmen, and others, who would remain

---

[11] Thornbrough, *Indiana*, 1.

[12] Ibid., 405–406.

professionally associated with Wilder throughout his working life. Many would even relocate to other parts of the country with Wilder after the war. One such Lawrenceburg man who became a business partner (in a partnership that lasted longer than the one Wilder had with Probasco) was David E. Rees, a Lawrenceburg farmer and, later, a banker. Thirteen years older than Wilder, Rees is mentioned frequently in correspondence between Wilder and his wife during the Civil War.[13]

Wilder's foundry in Greensburg, Indiana, flourished, as indicated in an 1861 letter Rees wrote to Wilder shortly after Wilder had joined the Union Army. Rees expressed unhappiness at having to handle their business by himself and mentioned additional business interests in Jeffersonville (which was likely in Indiana although both Ohio and Kentucky had a Jeffersonville at the time) and a mill in Peoria, Illinois.[14] In a letter from 1858, Rees writes to a man named John Calder and mentions a "Sterling Mill" (possibly a mill in Sterling, Illinois, north of Peoria), as well as liens in Peoria.[15] In a wartime letter to his wife, Wilder discusses a proposal to furnish a man in "Hodginville" (perhaps Hodgenville, Kentucky) some machinery and for her to let Rees handle it.[16] When a fire damaged their home in Indiana while Wilder was away in the war,

[13] It is also possible that Rees was a distant relative of Wilder or his wife, Martha. Wilder's obituary lists Rees's son, Wilshire Rees, as a pallbearer, and a "cousin of the deceased." Wilder's youngest daughter, Martha, was given the name Rees as her middle name, and a letter to Wilder in the early 1860s from David Rees mentions "Uncle Silas," who was Wilder's father-in-law, Silas Stewart.

[14] David Rees to John Wilder, 18 August 1861, John T. Wilder Papers, Indiana State Library (hereafter cited as ISL).

[15] Ibid., 25 October 1858.

[16] John Wilder to Martha Wilder, 23 February 1862, John T. Wilder Papers, University of Tennessee at Chattanooga (hereafter cited as UTC).

Wilder wrote his wife, "I do not know how I shall spare the money to rebuild with. I have sent to David [Rees] all my savings to pay claims against us, but I cannot bear to think that we have no home."[17] Rees would play a bigger role in Wilder's life after the war; in 1866, he became a partner in the iron company Wilder established in Roane County, Tennessee.[18] From these references to other Midwestern towns, it appears Wilder may have had foundries there as well, or at least was doing business there.

Another business partner, Antrim Riggs Forsyth, was from Greensburg, Indiana, and would also move to Tennessee after the war, becoming involved in Wilder's foundry business in Roane County. Forsyth is mentioned several times in wartime letters from Wilder to his wife, particularly in 1863 and 1864. He had been involved with the railroad business in Indiana and would stay with the Roane Iron Company until his death in 1892. Another Indiana businessman with whom Wilder developed a partnership was William Otis Rockwood. Wilder built up business associations in Indiana with several individuals who apparently saw in Wilder a man of success and means and who were willing to follow Wilder to the South when he chose to relocate there following the Civil War.

In the *Annals of the Army of the Cumberland*, Wilder is noted as having been "educated as a civil and hydraulic engineer." If this is true, he likely received that education, training, and experience in Columbus rather than back in the Catskills. This biography in the *Annals* states that Wilder had arrived in

---

[17] Ibid., 16 April 1863.

[18] Rees and his family moved from Indiana to Rockwood, Tennessee, at that point, and, in 1878, Rees moved to Chattanooga where he became instrumental in the founding of the Third National Bank. He died in Chattanooga in 1898.

Greensburg in 1852 and had "engaged in the machine and foundry business, in conjunction with his more scientific professional pursuit of hydraulic engineering."[19] The *Annals* biography also mentions that he became more "extensively engaged" in this field than any other man in the West and had mills, both steam and water, in many towns. The biographical sketch added that Wilder's interests spread to Illinois, Wisconsin, Virginia, and, curiously enough, Tennessee and claimed he owned several hundred acres of land there prior to the Civil War.[20] The *Annals* sketch goes on to add,

> He has built over one hundred mills, has sent engines (all built by contract) to every part of the West, has constructed several large hydraulic works, and has been granted three patents on turbine water wheels.... He had become proficient in hydraulics, and was recognized as an authority in such matters to so great an extent that he was sent for as a witness and to act as umpire from all parts of the country.[21]

Letters in Wilder collections in several archives do refer to other mills throughout the Midwest.

At some point in the 1850s, Wilder relocated to Greensburg, Indiana, and established a foundry. Greensburg, in the south-central part of Indiana in Decatur County, had been named for Greensburg, Pennsylvania, and was settled in the early 1820s. Shortly prior to that, the US government had taken the land from the Indigenous tribes in the region. Decatur County was then set up in 1821 and named for American naval hero Commodore Stephen Decatur (1779–1820). In spring 1822, a court was established and a local government set

---

[19] Fitch, *Annals*, 233–34.

[20] Attempts at verifying this have not turned up any land ownership by Wilder prior to the war.

[21] Fitch, *Annals*, 234.

up. The site of the county seat was chosen in June 1822 and named Greensburg. A little over thirty years later, it would be the location for Wilder's new foundry. Wilder was successful with this foundry, which was known to produce turbine engines, possibly of Wilder's own invention. The 1860 census lists Wilder's personal wealth as $25,600 (self-reported and possibly a bit lower than it was to avoid paying higher taxes), which, in early twenty-first-century comparisons, would equal just under $700,000. For a man just thirty years of age, he seemed to be on a very successful track, professionally and financially.

As a millwright and foundry owner, Wilder was resourceful in inventing machines, turbines, and other equipment necessary to operate his business. It was around this time that an innovation in foundry furnaces came about: the drop bottom cupola. The standard cupola, of which variants had been used for nearly two thousand years, was a furnace resembling a smokestack that was filled with layers of coke and ignited. As the coke burned, air would be pumped in through side entrances called *tuyeres*. When the coke became extremely hot, metal was added from the top of the cupola with more coke. As the mixture melted, it dripped into a pool at the bottom. The furnace master would monitor the amount of molten iron at the bottom and open a drain for it to flow into another container. After enough metal has been produced, the bottom of the cupola was opened and the remaining materials fell to a spot underneath, where it was removed after it cooled. As the early decades of the nineteenth century progressed to the 1840s, American foundries found that coal for heating produced better cast iron than the previously-used charcoal.[22]

---

[22] Chandler Jr., "Anthracite Coal and the Beginnings of the Industrial Revolution," 148.

The standard cupola, invented in Great Britain in the late 1700s, had been the standard melting unit for metal. Its usage in the United States dates back to 1815. Innovations around 1850 led to the development of the one-piece cupola, which led to air being better provided via blast tubes and air chambers. There is no record of whether Wilder took advantage of these innovations, but he was running a very efficient foundry at a time when innovations were increasing productivity. In the 1860–1861 city directory for Greensburg, as well as the directories for the nearby towns of Shelbyville and Rushville, Wilder's foundry is listed. An advertisement in the city directory promotes "Wilder's Involute Turbine Water Wheel," which Wilder patented in 1859. The ad describes the wheel:

> The wheels are made of either cast or wrought iron. When used under high falls of water, are made of steel, when an extreme amount of power is required from the smallest possible amount of water. They are guaranteed to utilize from 60 to 92 per cent. of the theoretical value of water—in proportion to the height of fall—high head sgiving [*sic*] higher per cent. than low ones. Iron Scrolls furnished when required. Back-water has no effect on them so long as the head is kept up. Ice cannot stop or injure them. There is one property possessed by these wheels that (to those accustomed to the use of other Turbines,) appears incredible; the wheels when working discharge but 59 per cent. of the area of the inlet or chute, and the faster they run the less water is discharged, being the reverse of all other Turbines. The wheel, when running without labor, discharging, but 42 per cent. of the area of inlet.[23]

Wilder, proactive in developing machinery for his business, had another 1859 patent, the horizontal water wheel,

[23] McEvoy, *McEvoy's Shelbyville*, 82.

described as "1st: constructing a water wheel with two sets of involute buckets, whose capacity shall be in the relative proportion to each other as specified. 2d, the combination, with a wheel such as has been described, of a casing provided with two channels of different capacities and with two gates, arranged as described."[24]

Today there is no trace of Wilder's foundry in Greensburg. Though records in Indiana archives and libraries, local and statewide, hold little information about this foundry, Wilder's business did prosper. He undoubtedly became an expert in hydraulics, and through his talents, work, and vision, grew wealthy for his labors and enterprise. Whether in one mill or others he may have owned simultaneously, it is said that he had more than one hundred workers in his employ by 1860.[25]

With his success and wealth growing, Wilder took the next step in adulthood—marrying and starting a family. At twenty-eight years of age and living in Greensburg, he married Martha Jane Stewart, who was seven years younger. Martha Stewart came from a prominent Greensburg family. Her father, Thomas Silas Stewart, originally from Pennsylvania, had been one of the earliest founders of Greensburg. The marriage took place on 18 May 1858, and in the ceremony Martha's half-brother Daniel also married. His wife was Martha Ann Tarkington, who would become the aunt of the prolific American author Booth Tarkington, who wrote *Penrod*, *Alice Adams*, and *The Magnificent Ambersons* and won the Pulitzer Prize for the latter two novels.

---

[24] Frazer, ed., "American Patents which issued in October, 1859," 35.

[25] The local library and historical society are well aware of Wilder's work and legacy in Greensburg, but unfortunately have been unable to acquire or preserve much on his prewar foundry.

Children came quickly for John and Martha Wilder. Their first child, a daughter they named Mary, was born nine months later, in February 1859. Family life would last only a few years, as growing tensions between the North and South eventually led to a major conflict in which men from all states would be called upon to leave their homes to work and fight in a civil war that would tear the nation, not even yet one hundred years old, apart.

Chapter 2

Enlistment and Early Service

John Wilder, now a family man and successful foundry owner, continued to run his foundry in Greensburg into the early 1860s. When hostilities broke out between the North and South in April 1861 and the nation appeared to be heading into a civil war, Wilder undoubtedly felt the call to duty. After all, his father, grandfather, and great-grandfather had all fought in previous American wars. Now Wilder saw his chance to do so and enlisted, despite the obligations of running his business and providing for his family.

The political situation in Wilder's state was changing. Indiana, in the 1850s, saw control by the Democratic Party shrink while the Whig Party strengthened to assist the new Republican Party to become the dominant party.[1] The Kansas-Nebraska Act of 1854, in which the territories that would become those new states could decide whether to allow slavery, was seen by many in Indiana as a betrayal of the Missouri Compromise, which had ruled against slavery in the Midwest regions.[2]

Although Indiana was not a slave state, there were citizens who may have been ambivalent in their feelings about slavery. By 1860, there were many former Southerners living in Indiana, particularly in the southern counties. Many had families, friends, and acquaintances with slaves in northern Kentucky, a slave state, just across the Ohio River. The prospect of secession and war with them made these Southern Indianans uneasy, if

---

[1] Thornbrough, *Indiana*, 45.

[2] Ibid., 54–55.

not resistant to war.[3] In letters to his wife during the war, Wilder speaks positively, for the most part, of Black people and Black workers; he also benefited from information received from Black citizens. He mentions that should his wife come to visit him at camp, that there would be plenty of Black girls to help her with the children. Several times he also recommended the prospect of using Black men as soldiers and did so again years later during the Spanish-American War. In an interview in 1898, during the Spanish-American War, Wilder suggests that Black soldiers could be used to fight in Cuba and that afterward Cuba could be a home for Black Americans, a proposal to relocate Black citizens outside the United States that can be construed as racist. After the war, when Wilder resumed his industrial work and other projects, he generally preferred and employed White workers over Black ones.

Whatever Indianans' attitude to slavery and the war, the state's men were quick to jump to their country's defense when news arrived of the attack at Fort Sumter. Many of these individuals, not just in Indiana but throughout the North, weren't specifically joining the ranks to end slavery but saw the Southern states' secession and the attack on Fort Sumter as an attack on their country's democracy.[4]

The day after the attack on Fort Sumter, two large meetings in Indianapolis took place, and from these came the resolve that Indiana would send men, as soldiers and officers, to answer President Abraham Lincoln's national call for seventy-five thousand volunteers. On 15 April, Indiana governor Oliver P. Morton also called for state volunteers to enlist and promised President Lincoln the state would provide ten thousand men. The United States—what remained of it after

[3] Barnhart, "Impact of the Civil War on Indiana," 186–87.
[4] McPherson, *Battle Cry of Freedom*, 308–309.

Southern states had seceded—would need Indiana's agriculture, railroads, and access to the Ohio River and the Great Lakes, which could be used to move armies and supplies. A fort was quickly built in Indianapolis for training and named Camp Morton, after the governor. By the end of April, six regiments had been formed. More than half of Indiana's volunteers trained at Indianapolis, but other camps were set up across the state.

Wilder was mustered in as a captain for an Indiana regiment on 23 April, only ten days after Union forces surrendered to Confederate forces at Fort Sumter. His joining the Indiana regiment would have involved taking an oath of allegiance and the reading of the articles of war, a lengthy document already several decades old. After that, Wilder would have undergone basic training where soldiers were taught to march and properly use their weapon. The efficiency in how these skills were taught varied, as the army had no systematic training program in place, with some officers teaching directly from a manual, which may have been William J. Hardee's *Rifle and Light Infantry Tactics for the Exercise and Manoeuvres of Troops When Acting as Light Infantry or Riflemen.*[5] Even though Hardee, a veteran of the Mexican-American War and a West Point graduate, had chosen to fight with the Confederacy, his manual was the most-used manual used by either side.

Leaving his family to join the army must have been difficult for Wilder. But early in the war, the excitement over the adventure (and assumption that there would be a quick resolution) spurred many to enlist. Wilder left behind a wife who was nearly nine months pregnant with their second child.

---

[5] Wiley, *Life of Billy Yank*, 24–25; Philadelphia: Lippincott, Grambo & Co., 1855.

Two weeks after being mustered in, on 6 May, Martha gave birth to another daughter, whom they named Anna. The same month, the thirty-one-year-old Wilder had his foundry cast two six-pound cannons and formed a light artillery company. The military mustered the company in on 12 June as Company A (one of ten companies, A–K) of the 17th Indiana Volunteer Infantry at Camp Morton. Most of the 17th Indiana soldiers were outfitted with either Enfield rifles or smooth-bore muskets. During June 1861, the regiment trained at Camp Morton. Meanwhile, other Union troops in the state were organized, and preparations began to move them to strategic positions further east.

Colonel Milo Smith Hascall, a businessman and former schoolteacher from Goshen, Indiana, was placed in command of the 17th Indiana. Like Wilder, Hascall was a native New Yorker. After moving to Indiana in his teen years, Hascall had attended West Point in New York, graduating fourteenth out of forty-three in 1852. After West Point, Hascall spent a year at Fort Adams in Rhode Island, but he resigned and returned to Indiana to work for the Michigan Southern and Northern Indiana Railroad and to work as an attorney and district attorney. Enlisting as a private, Hascall would see rapid promotions and by the end of April 1862 would be promoted to brigadier general.

Wilder had enlisted into a United States Army that was seeing its forces divided, with many officers and soldiers choosing to go with their home states in the South, which were seceding from the Union. In 1861, the United States Army had just over eleven hundred officers and approximately fifteen thousand soldiers. These numbers would be reduced as some of the officers and soldiers from the South would leave to join the newly formed Confederate Army. In fact, almost a third of the United States' Army officers serving in 1861 chose to fight for the Confederacy.

The United States Army's need to increase its numbers resulted in political appointments and promotions, some ill-advised as individuals who received appointments or promotions may not have been the best suited for the position. But promotions and appointments were necessary and often happened quickly, with some officers even jumping ranks. Such was the need for war time leadership. Brevet ranks, mostly temporary promotions, were common as well. Wilder, already a proven leader of men from his successful foundry in Greensburg, would see similar promotions though he didn't rise as quickly as Hascall. After being appointed captain of the 17th Indiana, he was quickly promoted to lieutenant colonel, passing over the subordinate rank of major. As a captain, Wilder would have held command of a company of infantry, or even an artillery battery of guns; he also would have had some administrative duties and the responsibility of leading a company into battle. The higher rank of lieutenant colonel was the second in command of an infantry or artillery regiment, so Wilder would have assisted the colonel in his duties and in leading the regiment during battle. In the event the colonel was killed or wounded, the lieutenant colonel would immediately assume command.

Being an Indiana unit, the 17th Indiana Regiment was assigned to the Department of the Ohio, which had been created in early May 1861. The Department of the Ohio was originally made up of regiments from Ohio, Illinois, and Indiana but soon had regiments from western Virginia (now the state of West Virginia), Pennsylvania, and Missouri added to it. It underwent several changes as other regional states were added or dropped and eventually included regiments from Michigan and Kentucky. When Brigadier General Don Carlos Buell was appointed head of the department in November 1861, succeeding General William T. Sherman, the name was changed from Department of the Ohio to the Army of the Ohio. Born in Lowell, Ohio, in 1818, Buell was a veteran of the Seminole War in Florida and the Mexican-American War. He was a West Point graduate (class of 1841), had served with distinction in prior service, and had been wounded in the Mexican-American War. At the start of the Civil War, Buell was sent to California, where he had been stationed in the 1850s, but he was summoned back early to assume command of the Army of the Ohio and promoted to brigadier general from his rank of lieutenant colonel. He would be promoted to major general in spring 1862.

In the South, many eager young men enlisted, believing the war would be a short, but exciting—and victorious—adventure. The Confederate Congress had, in February, established a War Department, and the Confederate states began drilling whatever volunteer militia companies existed. The newly formed Confederate Army was not without competent officers, many who had been officers in the United States Army, or West Point graduates, including Robert E. Lee.

It wouldn't be long before John Wilder saw military action. In early May 1861, with the war only weeks old, Confederate General Robert E. Lee, commander of the Virginia Confederate forces at the time, sent Colonel George Porterfield, another Virginian and a veteran of the Mexican-American War, to Grafton, Virginia, to recruit soldiers and to gain control of the Baltimore and Ohio Railroad. Colonel Porterfield had little success in recruiting, as this western region of Virginia had largely been against secession. At the same time, Governor William Dennison of Ohio recruited West Point–educated, and Mexican-American War veteran George McClellan to take charge of Ohio's militia, making him a major general in the Union Army.

General McClellan's appointment early in the war in 1861 made Confederate colonel George Porterfield nervous, fearing General McClellan might attack his troops while in Virginia. Colonel Porterfield reacted by having his troops destroy railroad bridges in the attempt to slow McClellan's troops. General McClellan sent additional troops into western Virginia, and Colonel Porterfield moved his troops fifteen miles south to Philippi, Virginia (now in West Virginia), in late May. On 3 June, in what would be the first clash of Union and Confederate troops in the war, albeit little more than a skirmish, Union forces attacked the resting Confederate forces at Philippi. Colonel Porterfield's Confederate troops had marched all night from Grafton and collapsed into disarray when attacked. There were approximately thirty casualties from both sides, with most being suffered by the Confederate army. Nevertheless, Union newspapers claimed a major victory. Because of this defeat, Colonel Porterfield was relieved from command and replaced by General Robert Garnett, another Virginian.

General Garnett immediately fortified two nearby areas: Belington (Laurel Hill) and Rich Mountain, which he viewed as a main gateway to the northwest. Confederate general H. R. Jackson, in command of the Confederate Army of the Northwest, set up his headquarters in Monterey (near today's Virginia/West Virginia border) and gathered the disorganized Confederates. His first task was to set about reorganizing the army and boosting their morale.

Because there were anti-secession and anti-Confederate sympathies in the western side of Virginia, the Union Army sent troops from Ohio and Indiana to that region to recruit

Virginians for the Union army. Included in this assignment was the 17th Indiana. On 1 July, their training completed, Wilder, with the 17th Indiana Regiment, left Indianapolis by train for duty in western Virginia. Along the way, they stopped for three days at Camp Clay near Cincinnati. The regiment, again traveling by train, then rode to Parkersburg, Virginia, arriving on 5 July. There, they set up a camp that they named Camp Hascall. Several days later the 17th Indiana marched twenty-three miles southeast in rain to Elizabeth, Virginia, where they joined with four companies of the Ohio 22nd , commanded by Colonel William E. Gilmore.[6] They remained at Elizabeth for two days and then received orders to march approximately thirty miles to Spencer, further south. By this time, Lieutenant Colonel Wilder was in command of 380 men of companies B, E, G, and K of the 17th Indiana. In one of his first exposures to combat, Wilder took 160 men, leaving the others with Colonel Gilmore, and traveled south on foot over the mountains toward Spencer, where approximately six hundred Confederate troops were encamped. Taking whatever path or trail they could find, roads being nearly non-existent in this area, they made a surprise attack on the Confederate troops. They killed one Confederate soldier, wounded another, and captured five Confederate soldiers and three horses, including a gray stallion that Wilder personally captured. Casualties on the Union side were slight, with only one of Wilder's men wounded. Wilder remarked in a letter to his wife that the Rebels

> did not dare to fight us fairly, but kept in the brush and on the hills, the route was very difficult, as the road wound through ravines and over mountains and around points

---

[6] John Wilder to Martha Wilder, 13 July 1861, John T. Wilder Papers, UTC.

> where they would lay in wait for us, but we kept flanking parties out ahead that came in behind them when they would run to some other point. The brush being so thick that our boys could not get a fair chance at them, we had this kind of work for about nine miles when they cleared out and we came on, and met Col. Gilmore's party just at the town...."[7]

Having run the Confederates off, they quartered in the courthouse in Spencer, and Wilder took over a lawyer's office in the building, calling his accommodation "first rate quarters." Not sure what their next orders would be, and even though they believed to be only twenty miles from Confederate forces that tripled theirs in number, Wilder was nevertheless confident they could defeat them, as he indicated in a letter to his wife.[8] With no further action ordered, they returned to Camp Hascall on 21 July.[9] On that same day, the war took a more serious turn as Union and Confederate forces clashed three hundred miles to the east, at Manassas, Virginia, approximately twenty-five miles from Washington, D.C. This was the first major battle of the war, which became known as both the first Battle of Bull Run and the Battle of Manassas.[10] Neither side was completely prepared for a battle because it was early in the conflict and troops were mostly inexperienced. The result was a Confederate victory and a wake-up call to Union forces that this war may not be over quickly. Both sides subsequently put

---

[7] Ibid.

[8] Ibid.

[9] *Compiled Records Showing Service of Military Units in Volunteer Union Organizations*, microfilm 38, National Archives and Records Administration, Washington D.C.

[10] The practice in the North was to name battles for the nearest body of water (e.g., Bull Run, Antietam, Stone's River) while the South typically named them after the nearest town or village.

out a call for more enlistments. (A second major battle at Bull Run would be fought just over a year later, again with a Confederate victory.)

On 23 July, the 17th Indiana proceeded by train to Oakland, Maryland, in the western part of the state. From there, on 26 July, they marched approximately sixteen miles east, to the north branch of the Potomac River to Camp Pendleton on the north branch of the Potomac River.

General McClellan sent General William S. Rosecrans to Rich Mountain and another Union force to Laurel Hill, southwest of Charleston, in mid-July. Born in Ohio, Rosecrans (or "Old Rosy" as he was nicknamed) was a graduate of West Point. He did not, however, serve in the Mexican-American War as West Point assigned him to duty in several eastern states during that period.

At the Battle of Rich Mountain on 11 July 1861, Union forces routed Confederate forces under the command of Lieutenant Colonel John Pegram. Pegram, a West Point graduate, surrendered his regiment and was out of the war for half a year until an exchange was arranged. He has the distinction of being the first Confederate officer who had previously been a Union officer to be captured by Union forces. After his exchange, Pegram continued to serve in the Confederate Army and was promoted to brigadier general in 1862. He would be killed in the Battle of Hatcher's Run in Virginia in February 1865, just weeks after marrying Hetty Cary, who had helped design the first Confederate flags.

The Confederate troops retreated south to Monterey and suffered the loss of General Robert Garnett, who had replaced Colonel George Porterfield. General Garnett was killed at Corrick's Ford near Parsons, Virginia (West Virginia). Confederate brigadier general Henry Wise had strategically positioned his troops in order to force Union troops back and was attacked by Union troops from Ohio under the command of General Jacob Cox. Wise and his men were able to stand their ground and hold them off.

Meanwhile, General McClellan had ordered Union troops under General Rosecrans sent to Beverly, Huttonsville, and Cheat Mountain Pass after the battle of Rich Mountain in Virginia. On 18 July, Union troops camped at the base of the mountain captured a small group of Confederate soldiers, whom they immediately paroled. By 23 July, they had a managed to set up a telegraph wire for communications, and by the end of the month, the 14th Indiana Regiment, under Colonel Nathan Kimball, was at the top of Cheat Mountain.

In late July, Rosecrans took command of the Union forces in Virginia, replacing General George McClellan, who had assumed command of the Division of the Potomac, which was renamed Army of the Potomac less than a month later. General Rosecrans placed Colonel Joseph J. Reynolds in command of the Cheat Mountain, Huttonsville, and Elkwater forces. Rosecrans's first charge was to have Union forces "occupy" rather than act as aggressors in the region.[11]

Previous area battles and skirmishes, such as Philippi, Rich Mountain, Carrick's Ford, and Laurel Hill, had been disastrous defeats for the Confederacy, especially in light of the loss of General Garnett. The victory at Bull Run stands out as the earliest success by the Confederate Army.

As General Robert E. Lee traveled to the area, he was accompanied by two aides-de-camp: Lieutenant Colonel John Augustine Washington, a grandnephew of George Washington, and Captain Walter H. Taylor. They first traveled to Staunton, Virginia, by train where General Lee met with

[11] Levering, "Lee's Advance and Retreat at Cheat River," 12.

General H. R. Jackson. The next day they all traveled on horseback to Monterey, and then to Huntersville, approximately thirty-five miles southwest. The Confederacy now had forces at Monterey and Huntersville, as well as Millboro. It was hoped that these forces could halt any Union troops' progress, including any by the troops on nearby Cheat Mountain.

On 7 August, the 17th Indiana proceeded west by train to Webster, Virginia (south of Grafton in what is now West Virginia), and then marched south approximately thirty miles to Huttonsville, reaching Cheat Mountain Pass on 12 August. From there they marched to Camp Elkwater, a camp that had been built by troops under command of Colonel Reynolds after the Confederates had been cleared from the area. This remote area offered nothing in the way of roads but required troops to travel through narrow trails over rugged terrain. At Camp Elkwater the 17th Indiana joined the 15th Indiana Regiment, and the 3rd and 6th Ohio Regiments.

On the Confederate side, General H. R. Jackson had been replaced by General William Wing Loring, who found himself face to face with Union forces commanded by Colonel Joseph J. Reynolds, of the 1st Brigade of the Army of Occupation of West Virginia. Colonel Reynolds's brigade included 377 officers, more than 10,000 men, and 26 pieces of artillery, spread out between Cheat Mountain, Beverly, and Elkwater. Most of the troops were from Ohio and Indiana, including the 17th Infantry regiment, still under the command of Colonel Milo Hascall. One regiment, the 23rd Ohio, included future president William McKinley. The nearby Confederate forces were made up mainly of the 7th and 16th Tennessee Infantry Regiments and the 1st Virginia Battalion Regulars. On 8 August, a Union scouting party of 150 infantry and cavalry captured two Confederate soldiers. No major fighting occurred, but the engagement saw brief periods of small skirmishes and guerrilla warfare, mostly between scouting parties on either side. Casualties were few.

General Robert E. Lee co-commanded the Confederate Army of the Northwest with General William Wing Loring, who had outranked General Lee in the US Army prior to the war. By the end of August, General Lee was promoted from brigadier rank to full generalship though the promotion had been confirmed by the Confederate Congress several months earlier. The relationship between Generals Lee and Loring was awkward, with Loring hesitant to report to a man once subordinate to him. On 8 August, General Lee traveled to Valley Mountain, accompanied by his son, William Henry Fitzhugh "Rooney" Lee.

General Lee directed Loring to advance on Huntersville and Monterey in early September and strike the Union troops at Cheat Mountain and Elkwater. General H. R. Jackson's force, the right wing of the Confederate army, had made it to the eastern base of Cheat Mountain. By this time, Union troops had built up defenses and gained strength. The 15th Indiana Regiment sent out a scouting party of 285 men toward the Huntersville-Huttonsville Pike but had orders not to engage Confederate troops, if avoidable. General Lee's main force was at Mace's Farm on Valley Mountain. On 9 September, Wilder and the 17th Indiana relieved the 6th Ohio Regiment, under the command of Colonel N. L. Anderson, at Point Mountain. The 17th Indiana had marched several hundred miles and was eager to see action since they had not yet encountered Confederate troops as they moved throughout western Virginia. By now Confederate troops were on the move, and General Lee was planning a major offensive with two thousand men by 11 September. Low morale due to rain and lack of rations hindered the Confederate troops' advance. Despite this, some Confederate troops under General Daniel D. Donelson moved further ahead than intended and found themselves exposed and in danger of getting cut off from the larger Confederate force. However, they had come across some Union pickets and captured them, getting from them information about Union positions.

General Lee's troops advanced near the Huntersville Pike, forcing pickets from the 15th Indiana and 6th Ohio to retreat. On 14 September, Confederate troops were in position in front of Elkwater but were soon forced to withdraw. The 17th Indiana was sent to open a path for communication and to clear the way for supplies, but they found the job already done. It was during this period Wilder began suffering something that would stay with him the rest of his life: dysentery.[12]

Sickness and disease were rampant in army life during war, and even officers were not exempt. Of the more than six hundred thousand soldiers from both sides who would die during the war, twice as many died of disease than from combat. Contaminated food and water in the camps and military prisons caused much illness and disease. Camps and prisons were frequently filthy and overcrowded, leading to the rapid spread of any contagion. Civil War physicians didn't yet know how infections originated or spread or how to create the sanitary, sterile conditions that are taken for granted today. Doctors, wearing dirty and blood-stained uniforms, would use the same instruments on one patient after another, often without cleaning and sterilizing surgical tools. Amputations of arms and legs, many possibly unnecessary, were common. Wilder's bout with dysentery would stay with him throughout the war, and even

[12] John Wilder to Martha Wilder, 26 September 1861, John T. Wilder Papers, UTC.

affect his life post-war. He would have periods of time during the war in which he was inactive, recuperating and dealing with his maladies, which would also include typhoid fever. As an officer, he would have received better treatment than the regular soldier, and he was also allowed, periodically, to go back to Indiana to rest and recover.

On 11 September, at the Huttonsville-Huntersville Pike, and the Point Mountain Pike, Generals Lee and Loring drove Union troops back, but the Union troops were quickly reinforced by the 15th Indiana. The 17th Indiana managed to escape on the Elkwater Fork Road but realized they had left two companies behind. Wilder organized a rescue party that found them and brought them safely back.

The troops of Confederate Generals Loring, S. R. Anderson, H. R. Jackson, and Colonel Albert Rust were well-entrenched in their positions. Union colonel Nathan Kimball, of the 14th Indiana Infantry, attacked Colonel Rust's position. By now Union forces totaled three thousand men on Cheat Mountain. Colonel Rust captured several Union soldiers, who, upon interrogations, inflated Union troop numbers to scare Colonel Rust, apparently successfully. As a result of this deception, Colonel Rust refused to advance further. Had he not believed them, a full-scale battle could have erupted, but with this turn of events, the Union would claim a small victory.

The Confederate forces would suffer one loss that bears mentioning during this encounter in Virginia. As the Confederate forces prepared to back down, General Lee's assistants—his son Major "Rooney" Lee and Lieutenant Colonel Washington—went on a brief foraging mission. Spotting a Union soldier in the distance, Washington advanced to capture him. Several Union soldiers from the 14th and 17th Indiana Regiments were in the vicinity as well, having been directed there by

Colonel Hascall, and took cover as they heard Washington and Lee approach. When the two men came into their range, the Union soldiers fired, hitting only Washington. In the melee, Lee managed to escape, but on Washington's horse. When the Union troops got to Washington, they found him still alive, but he had suffered three wounds in his back that exited out the front. Realizing the wounds as fatal, they helped Washington, giving him water at his request. Colonel Washington died from his wounds shortly after. Upon examining his body and his personal effects, Colonel Hascall realized who the deceased was. The next day, under a flag of truce, Colonel Hascall rode out with Washington's body to the Confederate camp. Major "Rooney" Lee and his escort rode forth to receive the body.[13] Confederate lieutenant colonel William Starke was quoted as saying, "Colonel Washington's temerity killed him; he was advised not to go where he did, but was on his first expedition, and extremely anxious to distinguish himself."[14] To the victors went the spoils, and some of Colonel Washington's personal effects were awarded to various 17th Indiana Regiment officers, including his gun, gauntlets, spurs, field glasses, and knife. The Battle of Cheat Mountain (if it can even be called a battle) was Wilder's and the 17th Indiana's first exposure to combat. It was a small victory for the Union, and the defeat for General Robert E. Lee damaged his reputation early in the war.

In the days following the Cheat Mountain campaign, the 17th Indiana set up camp at Elkwater, Virginia. Wilder continued to suffer from dysentery, but recurrences were usually short-lived. The 17th Indiana slipped into a period of idleness, which disappointed Wilder's men. During this time Wilder

[13] Some accounts credit Wilder with meeting personally with General Lee, but no official record gives this account.

[14] *Lewistown Gazette*, 2 October 1861.

was able to attend to domestic affairs and correspond with his wife and family. He received several shirts from his wife, which were no doubt much needed. In one letter, he requested two pair of woolen drawers "of homemade material if you can get it."[15] He gave camp news, including that Colonel Hascall was away on a two-week furlough. Wilder also noted in the letter, with disdain, that some Confederate troops had captured an entire Ohio company that had shirked its duties by going on a fishing expedition. Apart from this, their only action was an occasional skirmish and fighting back small forays from Confederate troops.[16]

On 3 October 1861, Colonel Reynolds, of the 10th Indiana Volunteers, led seven regiments into the Greenbrier Valley towards Camp Bartow, where General H. R. Jackson was preparing to set up winter quarters for his Confederate troops. After the Cheat Mountain campaign, the Confederate numbers were reduced, as many troops had been sent to reinforce the small Army of the Kanawha in the Kanawha River Valley. General Jackson had eighteen hundred soldiers camped at Camp Bartow, spread over only one mile. To Colonel Reynolds, this appeared to be easy pickings.

Reynolds began his assault by driving Confederate pickets back from the foot of Cheat Mountain. For this maneuver, the 17th Indiana led the attack, and Wilder advanced his regiment to within half a mile of the Confederate troops. He had the men form a line of battle in an open field. This would be the 17th Indiana's—and Wilder's—second battle. Wilder was again suffering from dysentery but was determined to be in this

---

[15] John Wilder to Martha Wilder, 26 September 1861, John T. Wilder Papers, UTC.

[16] Ibid.

campaign, apparently finding new strength as they approached the Confederate troops.

The battle commenced, and Wilder had his first brush with danger, narrowly escaping serious injury or possibly death as a twelve-pound Confederate cannonball flew over his head, close enough to blow his cap off. This same cannonball then hit the ground within ten feet of Colonel Reynolds, who was at the rear. Miraculously, Reynolds escaped without injury. Wilder's men were next ordered around a hill to within four hundred yards of the Confederate troops to provide support for Colonel Ebenezer Dumont's 7th Indiana troops. Wilder then called on his men to advance on the Confederate positions, which they dutifully, if not eagerly, did. They passed several Ohio regiments in disarray, and while being shot at by both musket and cannon, passed Dumont's 7th Indiana, also in shambles. Wilder was then ordered to halt, and they waited half an hour for further orders, but eventually they were pulled back. Colonel Reynolds then ordered the 17th Indiana to provide cover for the other regiments while they too fell back. Lieutenant Colonel William P. Richardson, of the 25th Ohio Volunteers, was then ordered to have his regiment advance and wait for the signal to charge. He got his men to the appointed spot and waited for the signal, which was to be evident when he saw charges by other Union troops. After a wait of almost half an hour, Wilder happened upon Richardson and told him he was to advance without any signal at all, and if he didn't do it, Wilder would. Richardson took Wilder's order and advanced his men. This was all for naught, as shortly the command was given for everyone to retreat. All of these advances and orders proved to be ineffective as most Union troops were marred with confusion, accomplishing little.[17]

According to Wilder, he kept his men in order and led the only regiment that was able to advance up the hill. Colonel Reynolds had his men cover the troops as they backed down from their positions.[18] By mid-afternoon the battle was over, with six Confederate fatalities and thirty-three wounded; the Union forces fatalities were eight, and thirty-five wounded. During this battle, the 17th Indiana lost one man. Wilder observed in a letter to his wife that the Confederate shells did little to hurt them, and that only one in ten burst; he supposed they forgot to cut the fuses.[19]

After the battle of Greenbrier River, the 17th Indiana remained idle in the area for several weeks. Wilder wrote to his wife from Huttonsville, Virginia, that "we have very dull times here now that the enemy have run away from us, we cannot get transportation to follow them, our brigade has fallen back from the mountains into the valley, leaving Gen. Dumont at Elkwater and Gen. Mulroy [*sic*] on top of Cheat Mountain."[20] He wasn't looking forward to spending the winter there and was hoping to get a furlough to come home for a month. However, his health was better, he also noted.[21]

On 19 November, the 17th Indiana was sent to Louisville, Kentucky, and reported to General Buell on 30 November.

---

[17] United States War Department, *The War of the Rebellion: A Compilation of the Official Records of the Union and Confederate Armies*, ser. 1, vol. 5, 222–23 (hereafter cited as *OR*).

[18] John Wilder to Martha Wilder, 5 October 1861 (transcription only), John T. Wilder Papers, UTC.

[19] Ibid.

[20] Wilder evidently meant Brigadier General Robert H. Milroy.

[21] John Wilder to Martha Wilder, 25 October 1861, John T. Wilder Papers, UTC.

They camped at the Oakland Race Course, a defunct racetrack now evidently used as a suitable camping ground, and stayed until 10 December. They were then assigned to General William "Bull" Nelson's Army of the Ohio's 4th Division, and then marched to Camp Wickliffe, near Hodgenville, Kentucky. During this period there was much disease and sickness, including smallpox, within the 17th Indiana. The disease was so prevalent that a convalescent camp was set up at Nelson's Furnace, near New Haven, Kentucky, approximately ten miles northeast of Hodgenville. The 17th Indiana remained at Camp Wickliffe drilling the rest of 1861 and into 1862.

Union soldiers found ways to pass the time, when not on the move or in battle. Letter writing was common, as this was the only way of keeping in touch with their families and loved ones. Soldiers looked forward to mail from home as well, especially if packages came with much-needed clothing, supplies, or sundries. Wilder seemed to get fewer letters from his wife than he expected; many of his wartime letters indicate his frustration at long periods of not receiving communications from home. Shopping at the sutler's store, which was set up to handle basic supplies for soldiers, was another pastime though these businesses often charged exorbitant prices for basic goods. Soldiers also passed the time engaged in games and sports. Card games (and gambling) were popular, and the fledgling sport of baseball also occupied the soldiers' free time.

Wilder developed pneumonia on New Year's Day. The conditions were dirty, like many camps, and Wilder, in a letter to his wife, proclaimed it the "unhealthiest camp I have ever seen, Western Virginia no comparison to it."[22] He was also still suffering from dysentery and, according to a military doctor, a

[22] Ibid., 18 January 1862.

"hemorrhage from the lower bowel," the phrase then for a bloody discharge.[23]

On 10 February, the 17th Indiana was sent south, through Bowling Green, Kentucky, arriving at Munfordville on 18 February, where they were placed under the command of General Thomas J. Wood, of the 6th Division of the Army of the Ohio.[24] Wilder still suffered from his various maladies, but wrote to his wife, "the prospect of a fight improves me still more."[25]

On 23 February, the day after Jefferson Davis was inaugurated for a full six-year term as the Confederate president (after serving for just over a year as the provisional president and president-elect), Union troops from the Army of the Ohio were sent to Nashville. With victories at Fort Henry and Fort Donelson, Union troops led by General Buell then occupied Nashville as Confederate forces left the middle section of Tennessee, resettling in Memphis. Thus, Nashville became the first Confederate state capital to fall. It would remain in Union hands for the remainder of the war, even surviving a major battle in 1864.

Like many other soldiers and officers, Colonel Milo Hascall had been ill during the late winter and was recovering at Louisville, tended to by his wife. The 17th Indiana was placed under the command of General George Wagner, another Indianan, but one for whom Wilder had little respect. Wilder would confide to others that he hoped to go to

---

[23] Ibid., 26 March 1862.

[24] Munfordville would later be the site for a major event in Wilder's Civil War career.

[25] John Wilder to Martha Wilder, 23 February 1862, John T. Wilder Papers, UTC.

Nashville, where he intended to plant the flag of the United States on the dome of the capitol.

The 17th Indiana was soon transferred back to General Thomas J. Wood. Wood, a native of Kentucky, was a cousin of Confederate general Benjamin Hardin Helm, who was married to Emilie Todd, half-sister to Mary Todd Lincoln, the current first lady. Wood was also a career Army officer and a veteran of the Mexican-American War. Wilder at this point believed the war would not last much longer.[26] The 17th Indiana moved into Nashville, camped at Edgefield Junction, and remained there until the end of March.

On 25 March, Wilder was promoted to full colonel and given command of the 17th Indiana, replacing Milo Hascall, who had been promoted to brigadier general the month before. One of his first assignments in command was in late March, as the 17th Indiana was sent south to Lawrenceburg, Tennessee, to clear out what was believed to be a small gang of Confederates. During this time, Confederate troops under the command of Generals Albert Sidney Johnston and Pierre Gustave Toutant Beauregard began moving towards General Grant's Army of West Tennessee, camped near Shiloh Church at Pittsburg Landing, Tennessee. After the recent Union losses in the battles of Fort Donelson and Fort Henry in northern Tennessee, Johnston was eager to get the advantage over Northern troops and to block them from moving into northern Mississippi. What transpired was the bloodiest battle to date on American soil, with many important military commanders involved on both sides: For the Union, Generals U. S. Grant, Don Carlos Buell, William T. Sherman, and Lew Wallace. For the Confederacy, Generals Albert Sidney Johnston, P. G. T. Beauregard, Leonidas Polk, and Braxton Bragg.

---

[26] Ibid.

Confederate troops surprised General Grant's army, but reinforcements primarily from General Buell's divisions helped turn the tide for the Union forces. For two days, 6 and 7 April, Union and Confederate forces fought in the massive battle known as the Battle of Shiloh or Pittsburg Landing. In the Union victory, General Albert Sidney Johnston was killed after being shot in the leg and bleeding to death while still engaged in the fighting. The 17th Indiana, moving from Lawrenceburg, Tennessee, approximately sixty miles east of Shiloh, hurried to get to the battle. They captured supplies and confronted small bands of Confederates along the way. After marching for ten days (and making up to twenty-seven miles each of the last three days), they arrived as the battle was ending. What Wilder saw shocked him, as he described the carnage in a letter to his wife:

> I will not attempt to tell you of the awful destruction on the battle ground which covered a space of about 25 square miles—the dead lay on every acre of it when we came here. There was just about two rebels for each one of ours—probably 9000 in all dead—hundreds of trees shivered to splinters, gun carriages torn to bits, dead horses by the drove, heads, arms, legs and mangled bodies strewn around, all combined to make up a picture of horrors that it would be well for our infernal political leaders to look on, and if they did not then learn to mind their own business, to be made a part of.[27]

Wilder's account of the number of dead was much higher than it actually was. However, this was Wilder's first exposure to the aftermath of a major battle, and he must have been horrified at what he saw. In all, approximately twenty thousand Confederate and Union soldiers and officers were killed or

[27] Ibid., 16 April 1862.

wounded during the battle of Shiloh. With such a large and bloody battle, both sides were beginning to realize that this war was not going to be over quickly.

Wilder's troops joined the Union advance the next morning on the retreating Confederate forces moving south to Corinth, Mississippi. The Confederates were led by Beauregard, who had assumed command upon the death of Johnston. Henry Halleck had sent word to General Grant to avoid further fighting until he had arrived and taken command. Halleck had replaced General John C. Fremont as the commander of the Department of the Missouri; he was an imposing figure, and his soldiers referred to him behind his back as "Old Brains" due to his expertise in military studies. This nickname was also used somewhat derogatorily.

During the aftermath of the battle, General William T. Sherman led a chase on the retreating Confederate armies but was surprised by a Confederate cavalry led by Nathan Bedford Forrest. Forrest's men inflicted a number of casualties on the lead regiment, the 77th Ohio. In this skirmish Forrest was wounded but survived. In the next several weeks, Union forces set up a slow advance on Corinth, making wooden "corduroy" roads as they proceeded. Joining them was General John Pope, commander of the Army of Mississippi, with approximately twenty-five thousand men. Wilder, who had hoped to leave the military at spring's end, found his plans changed with his promotion to the command of the 17th Indiana.[28]

The Confederate Army, upon reaching Corinth, began building fortifications and treating their wounded. Strategically, Corinth was an important location, as it was a junction for the Memphis and Charleston Railroad and controlled rail lines going north and south, as well as east and west. Union

[28] Ibid., 29 April 1862.

general Henry Halleck arrived at Shiloh on 11 April, several days after the fighting. Halleck had received positive reports on Sherman's performance in the battle, which elevated his status in Halleck's mind, but both Grant and Buell had yet to impress him. In fact, Grant and Buell didn't impress each other.[29] Many Union officers were slow to recognize and admit Grant's ability, particularly in light of his resignation from the Army in the mid-1850s to avoid a possible court-martial for drinking. President Lincoln, however, valued Grant. Having given the command of the Army of the Tennessee to General George H. Thomas, Halleck appointed General Grant as his second-in-command, most likely so he could keep Grant out of the picture and uninvolved.[30]

The Union forces waited for Pope's Army of the Mississippi to reach them before advancing on Corinth, only twenty-two miles to the south. Pope was prone to making bold and brash comments, but his big talk did not match his abilities. He was placed in command of the Army of Virginia, but, after his defeat at the second battle at Bull Run, he was sent to Minnesota to fight uprising Indians.

During the advance on Corinth, General Halleck preferred to outmaneuver the Confederates rather than engage them in battle.[31] General Halleck ordered his commanders to avoid engagements if possible and to keep their troops together, but during this tedious month-long march there were nearly thirty skirmishes. It wasn't a Confederate defeat Halleck wanted but, rather, Corinth itself. Mistakenly thinking the Confederates' numbers were similar to his own, General Halleck strove to emphasize order and discipline among the ranks.

---

[29] Engle, *Struggle*, 166–68.

[30] McPherson, *Battle Cry of Freedom*, 406.

[31] Woodworth, *Nothing but Victory*, 205.

Perhaps to boost morale, Halleck roughed it with the men by sleeping in a tent and eating the same food as the soldiers, an unusual move for an officer, particularly a general.[32]

On 29 April, General Halleck, with the Armies of the Tennessee, Ohio, and the Mississippi, began the slow march, with 120,000 men, including Wilder's 17th Indiana. In command were Generals John Pope, Don Carlos Buell, and George Henry Thomas. Moving with such a large force, entrenching daily, the slow march to Corinth took nearly one month, as they only averaged three quarters of a mile each day. As Union forces approached Corinth, Beauregard realized that he was outnumbered two to one, with many of his troops sick or wounded. Wanting to hold Corinth in order not to lose control of the Mississippi Valley, Beauregard managed to add reinforcements, eventually building his troop numbers up to seventy thousand. Nevertheless, Beauregard realized this was not enough and ultimately and quietly ordered his men to retreat further south in late May, only hours before Halleck and his men marched into Corinth.

Upon finding the Confederates gone, General Halleck sent a portion of his forces in a halfhearted pursuit, with the troops traveling five miles the first day, three the next, and then spent five days camping before they returned to Corinth. At this point, the 17th Indiana joined General Buell's forces and moved south through northern Alabama, then north to McMinnville, Tennessee. There they again encountered General Forrest and his troops, forcing Forrest to retreat.

In just over a year, John T. Wilder had enlisted in the Union Army and been promoted to colonel. By summer 1862, he commanded the 17th Indiana Volunteer Infantry, which until this point had seen action only in western Virginia (and only

---

[32] Engle, *Struggle*, 169.

in small battles), encountered small bands of Confederates, and participated in the slow march to Corinth, Mississippi. Wilder's health had suffered since enlisting, with bouts of dysentery and a period of typhoid fever. In late spring 1862, Wilder received a much-needed furlough to go home, rest and recover, and tend to his business and family affairs.

In June 1862, Wilder apparently had recovered enough to travel back to New York to visit his parents and siblings, some living in Samsonville, approximately six miles south of Olive. In a letter to his wife in Indiana, he reports that many friends came by to see him and that his family was much disappointed that she hadn't joined him on the trip. He also mentioned that he still felt poorly and had applied for an extension of thirty days' leave.[33] It was during this timc that evidence of Wilder's devotion to duty and his superiors is evident. A deserter from Hascall's regiment made a public accusation of cowardice against General Milo Hascall. In early June, Wilder sent a letter to General Hascall's hometown newspaper, the *Goshen (Indiana) Times*, repudiating this charge and labeling the deserter as a liar, forger, and swindler. He furthermore offered $30 of his own money for the deserter's capture.[34]

---

[33] John Wilder to Martha Wilder, 17 June 1862, John T. Wilder Papers, UTC.

[34] Bulla, *Lincoln's Censor*, 149.

Chapter 3

Surrender at Munfordville

While resting at home in Greensburg, Indiana, in July 1862, Wilder was well enough to recruit several hundred citizens from Decatur County in response to Governor Morton's call for new soldiers. The early response to the call for recruits in Indiana was strong. More men showed up to enlist than the government was prepared to handle, but they somehow managed. Volunteers arriving in Indianapolis received a hearty welcome and reception. By summer 1862, it was obvious to all that the war was not going to end soon. Enlistees were being recruited for three years' service rather than the original three months or a year. Still, there were plenty of enlistees from Indiana as the war progressed. There was pressure, of course, for all eligible men to enlist. Many undoubtedly were "shamed" into doing so when their brothers or friends enlisted.[1] Many thought it would be a short adventure and had little idea as to the horrors of war, the meager conditions they would be living in, the sickness and disease of the camps and prisons, and the scarcity of medical help should they be injured or ill.

Little did Wilder suspect what lay in store for him once his furlough ended. In late July, news of "marauders" in the state prompted several hundred more men to enlist, so Wilder and Colonel James Gavin of the 7th Indiana Volunteers (also home on leave) were appointed to take the new recruits, 480 in all, and make them ready for service. Wilder and Gavin accompanied the new soldiers to Evansville, Indiana, stopping briefly to muster them in at Indianapolis. Then the new

---

[1] Thornbrough, *Indiana*, 126.

recruits were given the basic training in which they were taught to march and to use their weapons, likely using the manuals of Winfield Scott or William J. Hardee. There was no standard for training throughout the armies, Confederate troops included, and the effectiveness of training was hit-and-miss throughout the military.[2] However, as these recruits had only enlisted for a thirty-day period to fight Confederate marauders in Indiana, led by John Hunt Morgan, their training may have been minimal.

On 25 August, Wilder and new recruits traveled by train from Indianapolis to Louisville, Kentucky. They remained there for two days before receiving orders to go to Nashville, now in Union control. Upon reaching the Red River Bridge near Clarksville, Tennessee, they found the railroad bridge destroyed by John Hunt Morgan's Confederate guerrillas, who had come into the state in advance of General Braxton Bragg's Confederate army. Morgan, a Kentuckian, had formed a Kentucky Confederate militia in early 1862, which fought in the Battle of Shiloh. By the end of that year, he was promoted to the rank of brigadier general. Perhaps best known for "Morgan's Raid" into Indiana and Ohio, he was captured in Ohio but soon escaped from the prison where he was held. He returned to service and was killed in September 1864 during a Union raid in Greeneville, Tennessee.

The Louisville and Nashville Railroad—the L & N—served an important role for the Union Army because it was the main supply route for Union forces in Kentucky. Therefore, the Confederate Army, which had three camps in southern Kentucky and headquartered in Bowling Green since fall 1861, made the railway line one of their main targets.[3] As a

[2] Wiley, *Life of Billy Yank*, 25–26.

[3] Engerud, *History of the Siege of Munfordville*, 1.

result, the Union Army, which had camps in the northern part of Kentucky, stationed guards at every railroad bridge on the L & N line in the state, to guard against damage perpetrated by Confederate soldiers. The bridge at Munfordville, in south central Kentucky, was along a particularly strategic supply route for Union troops, so having it damaged or destroyed could disable the Union Army's supply route for many months.

After the Confederates' demoralizing defeat at Shiloh, General Braxton Bragg replaced General P. T. Beauregard as the head of the Confederate Army in the western theater. Braxton Bragg (1817–1877) was a West Point graduate (graduating fifth of fifty in the class of 1837) and had distinguished himself in the United States Army during the Mexican-American War. A North Carolina native, he had served in present-day Oklahoma after the Mexican-American War, in what was then known as Indian Territory. In the 1850s, Bragg resigned from the army and settled down to run a sugar plantation in Louisiana, his wife's home state. During this period, he was a colonel in the Louisiana Militia. On 7 March 1861, he was promoted to brigadier general of the Confederate States Army. His service during the Civil War has been the subject of much scholarship, and his reputation, accomplishments, and style continue to be debated and disputed by historians. However, Confederate president Jefferson Davis liked Bragg and kept him in command until the Battle of Missionary Ridge in November 1863 and subsequently appointed him in early 1864 to the role of his chief of staff.

Confederate forces, after escaping Corinth, Mississippi, in spring 1862, had moved fifty miles further south to Tupelo, Mississippi, to avoid a confrontation with General Halleck's troops, which now numbered over one hundred thousand to the Confederates' forty-five thousand. General Halleck's troops included the 17th Indiana, commanded by Wilder, and part of Buell's Army of the Ohio, made up with units from Ohio, Indiana, and Illinois.

General Bragg continued to move his troops further south by train in early August, to Chattanooga, Tennessee. Traveling in a roundabout way, they took a route through Mobile and Montgomery in Alabama, and then to Atlanta. Bragg met with Major General Edmund Kirby Smith, and the two generals planned on advancing and taking control of central Tennessee and then moving north into Kentucky to recruit soldiers and take control of the state. In late August, Bragg began his march north, only to discover that Buell's Army of Ohio was in Nashville. Bypassing Nashville, General Bragg headed up the L & N turnpike towards Glasgow, Kentucky. General Buell soon had his men heading north as well, towards Bowling Green, Kentucky. The Union Army needed additional troops at a vulnerable bridge at Munfordville, Kentucky, north of Glasgow, to hold the bridge until General Buell's army could arrive. The job was assigned to Wilder and the green troops he was taking to Nashville.[4]

In addition to his new recruits, many who had yet to receive munitions, Wilder also had nearly two dozen convalescing soldiers, who were armed. Using these armed soldiers as skirmishers, Wilder was able to repulse some Confederate guerrillas as he and his men traveled by train to Bowling Green, where they were to join General Buell's troops. As soon as they arrived in Bowling Green, Wilder was summoned to Louisville and abruptly directed by General Horatio Wright, Governor Morton of Indiana, and Generals Charles C. Gilbert and Jeremiah Boyle to proceed to Munfordville, Kentucky, with his men. Wilder's orders were for them to hold and protect the

[4] Brown, "Munfordville," 247–54.

eight-hundred-foot bridge that crossed the Green River at Munfordville from the Confederates.[5]

With a population of approximately two hundred, the town of Munfordville is on the north bank of the Green River in south-central Kentucky and is situated among small, rolling hills. The town, which dates to the early 1800s, was originally a relay station on the Louisville-Nashville turnpike. Munfordville got its name from Thomas Munford, an innkeeper, and Andrew Jackson had stayed at his inn on his way to his inauguration in Washington in 1829. Upon their arrival there, one of Wilder's soldiers, a new recruit in the Indiana 67th, described the area as being "one of the poorest countrys that I ever saw" probably due to the severe drought that the region had suffered.

On 8 September, Wilder assumed the command of the small gathering of troops and fresh recruits at Munfordville. Joining them were the 67th Indiana Infantry; the 89th Indiana Infantry; Company H, 2nd Battalion, of the 18th United States Infantry; Companies C and K, of the 74th Indiana Infantry; sixty men—all unarmed—of the 33rd Kentucky Infantry; several guns of 13th Battery of the Indiana Light Artillery; and just over two hundred of his own recruits, who had not yet seen combat. In all, Wilder had 2,122 men to defend the bridge over the Green River at Munfordville. Their inexperience was not the only problem. Upon arrival in the area, Wilder's men had only one day's ration each. Wilder, ever resourceful, had his men forage the area to accumulate supplies and food to hold them for ten days. Helping them fortify the area were local Black citizens, possibly freed slaves, pressed by the government to assist. Wilder's men then went about strengthening an existing stockade, digging and constructing

[5] Williams, *Wilder*, 7.

more earthworks, and placed obstacles between them and the fields from where they anticipated the Confederate troops would certainly approach. In some areas they constructed earthworks as high as ten feet. Clearing trees to limit cover for the Confederate troops as they approached, they also created an abatis—obstacles from the downed trees and brush placed to slow the troops' advance. The stockade, which was named Fort Craig, was protected by six twelve-pound cannons. By this time, Wilder had learned that they were in the path of General Bragg's much larger Confederate Army as it swept into Kentucky from the south and headed north.

General Braxton Bragg sent Mississippi lawyer and politician General James R. Chalmers with his Mississippi troops to Cave City, Kentucky, to intercept and cut off Buell's communications to Louisville. After he arrived at Cave City, Chalmers learned that Wilder's troops were at Munfordville, only twelve miles away. Chalmers had already captured the telegraph operator and had taken possession of some depot supplies at Cave City, and the lure of what he thought to be an easy victory at Munfordville was too hard to resist.[6]

The Confederates were hoping to gain control of Kentucky, and both Bragg's and General E. Kirby Smith's Confederate troops had entered Kentucky from Tennessee. Smith, hoping to avoid being under command of Bragg (as did many others), agreed that he would not serve under him until their forces were joined. In the meantime, he would try to take the Cumberland Gap. Then, Smith and Bragg agreed, they would be able to take on General Buell's large Army of the Ohio. General Smith entered Kentucky in advance of Bragg, winning a battle at Richmond, Kentucky, in late August, which allowed him to occupy both Lexington and Frankfort. Bragg,

[6] Sykes, "Incident of the Battle of Munfordville," 537.

meanwhile, discovered that Buell's men were getting too close to Bowling Green for his comfort.[7]

General Bragg had set his sights on Louisville, hoping to meet up with General Smith. Unfortunately for Wilder, this destination would take Bragg and his army directly through Munfordville, where he was sitting with his small forces, including many raw recruits. On 9 September, Confederate troops under General John Hunt Morgan burned down the railroad bridge over the nearby Salt River. General Bragg's troops, advancing north, crossed the Cumberland River on 7 September at Carthage, with the intent of drawing Buell's troops into Kentucky. Meanwhile, Wilder was kept informed of their movements from reports of scouts.[8]

On 11 September, two Confederate deserters from General Simon Bolivar Buckner's command were brought to Wilder and told him that Bragg's troops were close and that General Buckner's division, with ten thousand men, including General Forrest's cavalry, was only seven miles away. General Bragg's army was believed to be as strong as fifty thousand men, with one hundred and four regiments, including eighty-four regiments of infantry, twelve batteries of artillery, and a cavalry of as many as ten thousand soldiers. Wilder's men continued to fortify the area, aware that support headed by Union General Lovell Rousseau was coming in from the south. This, wrote Wilder to his wife, disappointed him as he was looking forward to a "good, hard fight." Despite this apparent bravado, Wilder was a bit apprehensive of facing the Confederates with green soldiers and was looking forward to the arrival of his 17th

---

[7] Harrison, "Battle of Munfordville," 6.

[8] Hunter and Chamberlain, eds., *Sketches of War History*, 298. This six-volume work includes a chapter written by John T. Wilder, titled "The Siege of Mumfordville [*sic*]," and these references are from that chapter.

Indiana, on their way from Nashville, to reinforce them. Wilder knew that his situation was dire and indicated so in a letter to his wife, stating he would write more in a day or so, unless he was captured.[9]

As General Bragg's troops approached Glasgow, Kentucky, twenty miles to the south, Wilder's men could already hear them and worked faster to strengthen their positions. They dug several rifle pits in semicircles, giving them an advantage due to the topography of the area. In nearby Woodsonville, half a mile away, were the two hundred men of the 77th Indiana.[10] Wilder telegraphed J. Edward Stacy, the assistant adjutant-general and chief of staff in Louisville, for reinforcements and to confirm he was to hold the area. Wilder reported to Stacy: "Scouts and numbers of citizens coming in state that the enemy are advancing seven thousand strong, and that a force has come in between here and Bowling Green to prevent reinforcements from joining me." Wilder went on to ask if he could have reinforcements sent that night.[11]

General Bragg and his troops reached Glasgow on 12 September and blocked the L & N Railroad from General Buell's troops, currently at Bowling Green. The next day, Wilder learned that the Confederates had passed Glasgow and that another division of two thousand men of General Kirby Smith's forces was coming down the Green River towards Munfordville. That same day, Major General Charles C. Gilbert in Louisville directed the 50th Indiana, with five hundred men

---

[9] John Wilder to Martha Wilder, 12 September 1862, John T. Wilder Papers, UTC.

[10] Abbott would be killed in defending his position; his flag was pierced by bullets 146 times.

[11] McDonough, *War in Kentucky*, 159.

commanded by Colonel Cyrus L. Dunham, to proceed from Louisville to join Wilder at Munfordville.

The first Confederate troops to arrive at Munfordville were led by Colonel John Scott, with a brigade of three hundred. He demanded a surrender; Wilder refused. Scott then notified General Chalmers, who had come from Cave City on orders of General Bragg's commander of the Confederate Army's reserve division, Major General James Withers. Scott told Chalmers had been told that the Union troops at Munfordville were small in number and inexperienced and could be overtaken easily.[12] However, Chalmers quickly discovered from an intercepted telegraphic message that Colonel Dunham had been given orders to go to Wilder's position to reinforce him.[13] Anticipating that the Union forces would realize they were severely outnumbered and surrender on the spot, General Chalmers didn't notify his superiors that he was taking his troops to Munfordville. Upon arrival, Chalmers saw the Union fortifications and rifle pits overlooking the river, as well as an artillery bastion that could hold three hundred men. Nevertheless, he sent Lieutenant Colonel George H. Nixon forward under a flag of truce to demand the Union forces' surrender. Wilder, always the gentleman, entertained Colonel Nixon for several hours, no doubt discussing the situation and attempting to get as much information from Nixon as possible, before sending him back with the message that they would try to defend their positions, or as he put it, "we'll try fighting awhile."[14] Wilder then telegraphed Union headquarters at

[12] Noe, *Perryville*, 69.
[13] Brown, "Munfordville," 236.
[14] Benefiel, *Souvenir*, 62.

Louisville and told them he "peremptorily refused" the request to surrender.[15]

Confederate forces from Mississippi, led by General Chalmers, attacked at 5:00 the following morning, 14 September, using their artillery to drive the Union pickets back. Because of darkness and a heavy fog, General Chalmers could not see the Union fortifications or size of the Union Army. Nevertheless, he was still anticipating an easy victory. Members of the 67th Indiana were situated in an earthwork on Wilder's left, and to his right was the 89th Indiana. The rest of the men were in the newly dug trenches.

The Union forces held off firing until the Confederates had moved in close. General Chalmers's men advanced to within seventy yards of Wilder's blockade and took cover behind logs, receiving heavy fire from the Union troops. The stockade had a strategic higher vantage point, surrounded by rifle trenches and the rifle pits Wilder had his men dig. At daybreak, the Union forces withstood another attack on their south side, and Wilder sent members of Company K of the 74th Indiana to give assistance to their pickets in that area. At 6:30 a.m., Confederate troops began another advance, and Wilder, anticipating a ground attack, ordered his men to fix their bayonets. As they did so, members of the 7th and 10th Mississippi and the 7th Alabama, also with bayonets fixed, charged, thinking the Union troops were retreating. When they came to within thirty yards of their works, Wilder ordered his men to fire, unleashing a lethal fusillade of lead toward the attacking Confederates. Many Confederate soldiers were hit, causing mass confusion, panic, and then a retreat to the safety and cover of the nearby woods. Another similar charge was made, this time by the 9th and 29th Mississippi, and they met

[15] Harrison, "Battle of Munfordville," 8.

the same fate as their comrades. Wilder's men held their ground for more than five hours, but at 9:30 a.m., under another flag of truce, his surrender was again solicited. Realizing that the Union forces were too entrenched to be overtaken easily but knowing that a huge number of Confederate reinforcements were on the way to support them, General Chalmers hoped that Wilder might yet see the sense in surrendering to prevent the deaths of many soldiers.[16]

In a letter to Wilder, General Chalmers requested an unconditional surrender, despite a "gallant defense on your position," as he noted. He added that they were outnumbered and surrounded, making an escape or reinforcements impossible. Wilder's saucy reply: "Your note demanding the unconditional surrender of my forces has been received. Thank you for your compliments. If you wish to avoid further bloodshed keep out of range of my guns. As to re-enforcements, they are now entering my works. I think I can defend my position against your entire force; at least I shall try to do so."[17] Wilder did indeed receive reinforcements of nearly five hundred men, under Colonel Cyrus L. Dunham of the 50th Indiana, and others from the 78th Indiana. Wilder had been counting on these reinforcements from Louisville. Colonel Dunham's troops were able to get through despite having their train derailed six miles from Munfordville. Confederate forces had damaged the tracks, causing the train to derail and tip over, but the Union troops surprisingly suffered no injuries. Quickly organizing his troops for a possible ambush that never materialized, Colonel Dunham then marched his troops at double pace towards Munfordville, taking care to avoid any Confederates in the area. By taking cover in nearby trees, as well as cornfields and

[16] McDonough, *War in Kentucky*, 169.
[17] *OR*, ser. 1, vol. 16, pt. 1, 961.

ravines, Dunham's men managed to slip through the Confederate guards, drawing fire as they made it into the camp, to cheers from the Union troops already there. Upon arrival, Colonel Dunham could have assumed command, as per the directive of General Gilbert. However, thinking it unwise to change command in the middle of a battle, he deferred until the next cease-fire and planned to assume command the following morning. By this time, Confederate troops in the area had spread out, some planning on meeting General Buell's advancing army, and others guarding against any Union forces making an escape from Munfordville.

In an attempt to acquire additional provisions, Wilder had a locomotive repaired and sent to Salt River in hopes General Gilbert would provide him with supplies and ammunition. Afraid that the supplies would fall into enemy hands, General Gilbert declined the request.[18] General Gilbert told Wilder to hold on as long as possible and that General Buell with his troops would be arriving shortly.

Wilder's reply to the second request for surrender included the following: "Tell General Chalmers that I have excelled him in fighting; I can also excel him in courtesy. You can leave your flag on the field, bury your dead and remove your wounded until 2 p.m."[19] After a few more shots were fired (due to the slow progression of the truce news being received in various parts of the battlefield), each side managed to conduct its business of treating the wounded and removing the bodies of dead soldiers. Both sides briefly dropped hostilities. Confederate troops even borrowed tools from the Union side to bury their dead.[20] Two officers, one Union, the other Confederate,

---

[18] Hunter and Chamberlain, *Sketches of War History*, 297.

[19] Benefiel, *Souvenir*, 63.

[20] *OR*, ser. 1, vol. 16, pt. 1, 977.

met and conferred, even sharing brandy.[21] Some soldiers from the 89th Indiana went as far as to take some wounded Confederate soldiers to the Confederate hospital nearby.

Wilder's men had held their ground, but they were by no means out of trouble. General Bragg and his full army had yet to arrive at Munfordville, and Bragg was angered when he heard that General Chalmers had made an attack without orders, and even worse, had not yet been victorious. Furthermore, General Bragg was angered at the loss of an officer during the fighting—Colonel Robert A. Smith. The attack on the Union troops by General Chalmers was, Bragg would later write, "unauthorized and judicious."[22] Indeed, General Chalmers was now beginning to realize he had bitten off more than he could chew.

General Bragg's troops, camped at Glasgow, had been given the day off to rest, and many either attended religious services or drank themselves senseless.[23] General Bragg knew, correctly, that he could easily overrun the small Union army dug in at Munfordville. Bragg gathered his troops on 14 September and marched them post-haste thirty miles toward Munfordville. With him were Generals William J. Hardee, Leonidas Polk (the fighting Episcopal bishop and a West Point graduate), and Simon Bolivar Buckner. Buckner was a native Kentuckian (and a future Kentucky governor) who had been born near Munfordville. Not being from a seceded state, he had considered a commission with the United States Army at the onset of the war. Nevertheless, he went with the Confederacy and had been the first Confederate general to surrender an

---

[21] McDonough, *War in Kentucky*, 170–71.
[22] Ibid., 172.
[23] Noe, *Perryville*, 70.

army, which he did at Fort Donelson earlier that year, when he surrendered to Ulysses S. Grant.

As they approached Munfordville, Buckner convinced Bragg to surround the Union forces, rather than engage them head on. This may have been Buckner's effort to save his small hometown from further destruction from battle. On the morning of 15 September, they were all ready to engage—or accept the surrender of—Colonel Dunham (now in command, as the senior officer) and the several thousand Union troops.

General Hardee's troops positioned themselves on the south bank of the Green River while General Polk's men set up at the rear of the Union troops. In the ensuing exchange of letters and notes between Wilder and Confederate officers, the tone was always one of mutual courtesy. Messages ended with "respectfully yours," and "your obedient servant," as well as expressions of gratitude for small courtesies and promises of reciprocation, as was the custom of correspondence of the time. Wilder and General Chalmers originally arranged a "gentleman's agreement" that they would not fire upon any of the buildings in Munfordville or nearby Woodsonville. However, they still could, and would, express disagreeing viewpoints or air complaints or grievances. In one case during a cease fire, a Union sergeant assisting a wounded soldier was taken prisoner by Confederate troops. Wilder demanded his return. In an exchange between General Bragg and Wilder, Wilder complained that Confederate forces were "planting batteries" nearby during the ceasefire, a move Wilder insisted was contrary to "all rules of honorable warfare." He asked this to cease. General Bragg's reply was that the agreement had been that as long as the troops kept within their lines, no *gunfire* would take place, noting that this condition was being met.[24] Again, they

[24] *OR*, ser. 1, vol. 16, pt. 1, 970.

end their notes with the usual "respectfully yours" and "your obedient servant."

During this time, Colonel Wilder and Colonel Dunham had been attempting desperately to get more reinforcements, sending telegraphs and messages to General Buell, who was still approximately fifty miles away at Bowling Green. They were only then beginning to realize that General Bragg's army might even be larger than they first thought. So far, their standoff had been successful; they had lost only several dozen killed or wounded, compared to several hundred casualties for the Confederates.[25]

The Confederates made another attack on 16 September, and the two sides fought through the day with no advantage to either side. Again, the Union troops held their position. Late in the afternoon, the small Union army received another demand of surrender, this time directly from General Bragg, who again informed the Union officers that his army heavily outnumbered the Union forces. General Bragg gave them until 9:00 that evening to reach their decision. After conferring with the officers and staff, Colonel Dunham declined, sending Wilder personally to inform General Bragg of the decision. Then Colonel Dunham called a council of war with his officers. Several of the Union officers, though, were still not convinced General Bragg's army was as large as reported.

Colonel Dunham telegraphed General Gilbert at Louisville and informed him of their situation and that they would attempt to stand their ground. Gilbert's reply was for Dunham to turn over command to Wilder, an order that perplexed Dunham and one he felt unjustified, since he outranked Wilder.[26] Wilder, Dunham, and the other officers continued to

---

[25] Ibid., 962.

[26] Ibid., 966.

discuss the situation and concluded that continued fighting with the Confederate forces would be disastrous, given now that it appeared that Buell's forces would not make it in time, or perhaps were not even planning on coming to their aid. First, though, they would ask for proof that Bragg's numbers were as large as they claimed. It was at this point that Colonel Dunham turned over command to Wilder, as directed by General Gilbert. Dunham then telegraphed Gilbert, stating he was unwilling to serve under a junior officer and that he would go into the trenches and fight as a regular soldier. General Gilbert telegraphed back that he was to report to Colonel Wilder and have Wilder place him under arrest.[27] But shortly after directing Dunham to report to Wilder, Gilbert issued another order rescinding his earlier order for Wilder to take command and placing Colonel Dunham back in charge. However, for reasons unknown, this order was never received.[28]

Wilder, again in command, then requested from General Bragg proof of his superior numbers and even more amazing—a tour of Confederate forces so he could see for himself that they were indeed outnumbered. General Bragg, dumbfounded and unwilling to negotiate a surrender, replied, "The only evidence I can give you of my ability to make good my assertion of the presence of a sufficient force to compel your surrender beyond the statement that it now exceeds over 20,000, will be the use of it."[29]

Wilder, with his back to the wall and fearing the worst, next tried an unorthodox approach. Under a flag of truce, Wilder was taken into the Confederate camp to General Buckner. Having been assured that Buckner was a fair man and a

---

[27] Ibid.

[28] Ibid., 967.

[29] Ibid., 970.

gentleman, Wilder astonished him by asking advice as to what he should do, pleading a lack of military training. With his West Point education, Buckner immediately told Wilder that this sort of communication was not how wars were fought. However, Buckner quickly warmed to the idea—and to Wilder. "I wouldn't have deceived that man under those circumstances for anything," he would write later of the situation.[30] Reiterating what General Bragg had told Wilder, Buckner told him that it was indeed futile to continue to resist, but he did add this bit of counsel:

> No, Colonel; you appealed to me, and I must tell you frankly everything that I think a soldier ought to do. You need not tell me the strength of your army; I know what it is. You need not tell me that, because it would be wrong, but I know pretty well what it is. You are the judge of whether you could live under the fire that is to be opened on you; but if you have information that would induce you to think that the sacrificing of every man at this place would gain your army an advantage elsewhere, it is your duty to do it.[31]

Wilder then asked General Buckner for a personal inspection of the Confederate troops to ascertain their size, and Buckner readily agreed.[32] Wilder, still under a flag of truce, received a tour of the Confederate forces at Munfordville and saw that their numbers and weapons were as he had been told. And worse, the small Union army was completely surrounded. General Buckner next took Wilder to see Bragg, around midnight. They found Bragg writing in his headquarters, and, at first, General Bragg did not acknowledge Wilder's presence. Finally,

---

[30] Morton, "Last Surviving Lieutenant General," 85.

[31] Ibid.

[32] Harrison, "Battle of Munfordville," 45–46.

after he finished writing, he snapped at Wilder, "What do you want?" Buckner spoke for Wilder, giving Wilder's conditions for surrender: immediate parole, with personal effects returned as well as four days' rations; giving up all arms, ammunition, and government supplies; and his men paroled and sent home. Bragg adamantly refused, telling Wilder he had the force to completely destroy them. "No modification of the proposed terms will be made, and, if they are not accepted, I will kill every one of them when I open with my guns in the morning."[33] Wilder responded to General Bragg, stating that he didn't suppose that Bragg intended to waste all his ammunition on them, especially since General Buell was in the area with his army. Bragg dismissed Buckner and Wilder. Outside, Buckner exclaimed that this all was "willful murder" and bid Wilder wait while he went back in to discuss the situation with Bragg.[34] Thirty minutes later, General Buckner came back out and informed Wilder that General Bragg had decided to let him, Buckner, handle the surrender.[35]

Wilder, General Buckner, and General Bragg next spent several hours discussing the surrender terms, and it appears that the Confederate officers acquiesced to Wilder's requests. Rather than General Bragg's army marching victorious into the Union camp, Wilder negotiated that the Union troops would march out "with all the honors of war, drums beating and colors flying."[36] At 2:00 a.m., 17 September, the Union forces officially surrendered. Taken were 3546 men, enough tents for

---

[33] Sykes, "Incident at the Battle of Munfordville," 542.

[34] Years later, when Buckner was governor of Kentucky, Wilder would be a guest at a dinner at Buckner's governor's mansion and no doubt relived this occasion with Buckner.

[35] Hunter and Chamberlain, *Sketches of War History*, 302–303.

[36] McDonough, *War in Kentucky*, 181.

one regiment, a day's rations for the men, and ten pieces of artillery. General Bragg wrote to General Samuel Cooper, adjutant and inspector general of the Confederate Army, that they had also captured four thousand small arms, as well as artillery and munitions in the surrender. General Bragg also indicated that this victory came at the price of three hundred Confederates killed and wounded; however, he added, "My position must be exceedingly embarrassing to Buell and his army. They dare not attack me, and yet no other escape seems to be open to them."[37]

In his official report, General Chalmers stated that he was misinformed initially as to the numbers of Union troops and as to the likelihood they would not be able to receive reinforcements. He also blamed poor communications for not knowing the Union forces were better fortified than he thought, accounting for the number of losses Confederate forces suffered in attempting to overtake the Union forces.[38]

While Wilder had attempted to hold off General Bragg's army, Buell's troops foraged around Bowling Green, waiting for General George H. Thomas's troops to arrive. When Thomas's troops did arrive, Buell then marched towards Glasgow, thinking Bragg's Confederate army would still be there, only to hear along the way that they had indeed moved north to Munfordville.

Union general Don Carlos Buell would take criticism for not attacking Bragg's army and for not coming to Wilder's aid. These decisions generated some talk within the Union army, specifically that he was afraid of fighting Bragg's army. In explaining his not engaging Bragg at Glasgow, Buell would later claim that he would not have made it to Glasgow before Bragg

---

[37] *OR*, ser. 1, vol. 16, pt. 1, 968.

[38] Ibid, 972.

had passed through and therefore would have missed him anyway. General Buell also claimed that he had erred in thinking General Bragg would not move north to Munfordville, which would have lost him communications with Tennessee. Buell had believed that General Bragg's army was firmly entrenched and that it was more important for him to get to Louisville, rather than to fight Bragg's army at Munfordville. Ever cautious, General Buell also felt that his men were not ready and did not have the discipline to engage in a major battle, as a confrontation with Bragg's army was sure to be.

General Buell would also be criticized for letting Wilder's men be captured while he was in the vicinity.[39] Buell's reputation was not stellar to begin with. It was said that he never reviewed nor spent time with his troops and that few of his men had ever even seen him. This incident would mark the beginning of the end for General Buell; President Lincoln would soon replace him with General William S. Rosecrans as the head of the Army of the Ohio. Several weeks after Wilder's Munfordville surrender, Buell's action at the Battle of Perryville further damaged his reputation. Even though it was technically a Union victory, his slow response at Perryville and his subsequent refusal to give serious chase after the retreating General Bragg (Buell preferred to head toward Nashville) convinced Lincoln that General Buell was unfit to command.[40]

The Union soldiers at Munfordville marched out of their camp with agreed-upon haversacks, blankets, canteens, and four days' rations. Wilder handed over his sword to General Buckner, who, after officially accepting it, returned it to him. (Years later, Wilder would be a guest of Buckner when the latter was governor of Kentucky, and they certainly reminisced

---

[39] Daniel, *Days of Glory*, 119–22.

[40] Ibid, 126.

over the event.) The soldiers were paroled the next day and allowed to keep a cracker and a third of a pound of bacon from the rations captured from them. They were marched out between lines of Confederate troops to a band playing "Dixie."[41] They marched to Bowling Green but met up with Buell and his army first, and Wilder gave his impressions of Bragg's army.[42] Afterward, they entered Indiana, crossing the Ohio River at Brandenburg. North of Louisville, in Jeffersonville, Indiana, the troops then traveled by train to Indianapolis, where they were officially paroled.

This surrender and capture had taken place early in the war, at a time when paroles and exchanges were more common than actual imprisonment. Both sides, thinking the war would be over quickly, initially did not plan for constructing prisons or holding large numbers of prisoners. The United States at first refused to even discuss the issue of prisoners and prisons with the newly formed Confederate government, fearing such negotiations would legitimize it, after first refusing to acknowledge or recognize the new government. But by summer 1862, Confederate general D. H. Hill and Union general John Adams Dix created a plan for paroling and exchanging soldiers and officers to be practiced by both sides. The agreement was that soldiers were equally exchanged, one for one; noncommissioned officers could be exchanged for two soldiers; a second lieutenant could be exchanged for three soldiers, and this method would go up until a commanding general was worth sixty soldiers. Officers had to take a pledge not to escape or fight captors while awaiting exchange, whether in captivity or at home. There was little leniency for violating this agreement as it was decided that death by firing squad would be the

---

[41] High, *History of the Sixty-Eighth Regiment*, 16.
[42] Noe, *Perryville*, 76.

consequence of such an action. Waiting for an exchange was no picnic as holding camps for captees were soon overcrowded and unsanitary, not much better than the full prisons that soon were established.

This exchange plan had been in effect for several months when Union and Confederate forces met at Munfordville, but the plan would eventually break down as both sides quibbled and accused the other side of not being truthful and honest over helping soldiers and officers. Plus, Confederates would not treat Black Union soldiers with the same understanding and would either return them to their owners if they were found to be escaped slaves or just shoot them on sight.

The long march through Kentucky for the paroled Union soldiers was no easy task, but, once they were in Indiana, they found the citizens more willing to give them food and support. When they rejoined Union forces, however, their rations were hardly better than what they had before being captured.[43] Wilder, as an officer, was not paroled immediately, but he was allowed free access throughout the Confederates' camp for several days. He took advantage of this opportunity, making mental note of things he observed, such as the absence of trains of provisions or wagons with ammunition, and he met the officers of the Confederate troops.[44]

When he was released by the Confederates, Colonel John T. Wilder was a paroled prisoner of war and as such would be inactive from the war for a designated period or until exchanged. During his period of inactivity, he spent time in several places, including Indianapolis and Cincinnati, where on 11 November, he submitted a report of his regiment's activities

---

[43] Ibid.

[44] *OR*, ser. 1, vol. 16, pt. 1, 208–209.

for 1862.[45] One may also assume that he also spent time at home in Greensburg, looking after his business interests.

On 24 October 1862, the Army of the Ohio, which included Wilder's 17th Indiana, was restructured and became the Army of the Cumberland. Its territory was Tennessee and parts of Alabama and Georgia. Marching through the Kentucky towns of Lebanon, Columbia, and Glasgow, and into northern Tennessee, the 17th Indiana, without Colonel Wilder, arrived at Nashville on 26 November. In early December they went to Gallatin, Tennessee, approximately thirty miles northeast of Nashville. There they joined up with General J. J. Reynolds's 5th division of the 14th Corps of the Army of the Cumberland.

---

[45] Military document, 11 November 1862, Decatur County file, Greensburg-Decatur County (Indiana) Public Library.

Chapter 4

Winter 1862 and the Spencer Repeating Rifle

In December, at Washington D.C., Wilder procured an exchange with the Confederates and was subsequently directed to report to General William Rosecrans's army in Nashville, where General Joseph J. Reynolds was now commanding the 5th Division of the 14th Corps. Having served together the year before in Virginia, Wilder and General Reynolds were familiar with other. Upon arriving, Colonel Wilder was given command of a brigade made up with his 17th Indiana, as well as the 72nd and 75th Indiana, the 18th Indiana Battery of Light Artillery, and the newly formed 98th Illinois. Soldiers of the 72nd Indiana felt being added to Wilder's Brigade was an insult to Colonel A. O. Miller, whom they respected and felt had commanded them well in the previous months.[1] The 75th Indiana would soon be replaced by the 123rd Illinois, and the 92nd Illinois joined in 1863.

In November, Confederate president Jefferson Davis had appointed a recovered Joseph E. Johnston (wounded in the Battle of Seven Pines in Virginia in the late spring) as commander of the new Department of the West. Johnston would inherit a problem familiar to General Braxton Bragg, which was the increasing insubordination of officers, as well as the awkward situation of a native Northerner, John C. Pemberton of Philadelphia, being in charge of the Army of the Mississippi. President Davis complicated matters by ordering seventy-five hundred men transferred from Bragg's troops to Pemberton's.

---

[1] McGee, *History of the 72nd Indiana*, 84.

This move pleased neither Bragg nor Johnston, who feared General Rosecrans would take advantage of their weakened numbers to attack. President Davis valued Vicksburg more than middle Tennessee.

In a letter to his wife, Martha, on 15 December, Wilder wrote from Nashville that his health had improved. He mentioned sending home a Confederate sword he acquired from a fallen soldier and a Texas Ranger's saddle from one of General Forrest's men. Wilder also remarked that he wanted her to write more often and apologized for what Martha had perceived as criticism over her handling of their young children while he was away. "I know they are hard to manage and nothing but strict rule will keep control of them," he wrote, "but do not get discouraged, I will be home one of these days to assist you."[2] Wilder closed by boasting that his regiment was now the largest in the division and that General Rosecrans complimented them by stating they were the best "in all particulars" that he had seen.[3]

In Special Field Orders No. 23, the 17th Indiana, on 18 December 1862, was transferred from the 15th Brigade, 6th Division Left Wing to the 40th Brigade, 12th Division Right Wing by command of General Rosecrans. Two days later they received orders, in Special Field Orders No. 25, to proceed by rail back to Gallatin, Tennessee, and to report to General George H. Thomas.[4]

On 20 December 1862, Wilder testified to a commission in Nashville on his capture at Munfordville in September then

[2] John Wilder to Martha Wilder, 15 December 1862, John T. Wilder Papers, UTC.

[3] Ibid.

[4] *Special Field Orders No. 23*, 18 December 1862, John T. Wilder Papers, UTC.

officially took command of his unit on 22 December.[5] Wilder carefully chose trustworthy members of his 17th Indiana regiment to serve on his staff. The surgeon was Dr. Samuel Munford, his adjutant was First Lieutenant Greenberry Shields, and his ordnance officer was John T. Drury.

General William Stark Rosecrans had taken over the Union Army of the Cumberland in October and immediately began pooling supplies and preparing the troops in middle Tennessee for an advance. The day after Christmas 1862, Rosecrans began his move south out of Nashville.

While this went on, Wilder's men set out in a cold rain, heading north out of Nashville, Tennessee, once again chasing Confederate General John Hunt Morgan and his men. Marching was hard as they moved in the cold rainy weather, many with worn shoes and boots. In dealing previously with General Morgan, Wilder had observed the efficacy of movement and travel that General Morgan and his mounted soldiers could accomplish on horseback. As a result, Wilder decided to mount his men to give them an equal advantage and obtained permission from General Rosecrans to procure enough horses to do so.[6]

On 29 December, Wilder and his men were again in Kentucky, at Glasgow (bringing Wilder back near Munfordville), where they stayed for two days. On 30 December, Wilder allowed the men to forage, being out of rations. Their foraging was a success as the men brought in hogs, chickens, corn meal, flour, and applejack whiskey.[7] The latter supply resulted in a drunken festival as most of the men were reported to have freely consumed the liquor. In his history of the 72nd Indiana

---

[5] Baumgartner, *Blue Lightning*, 29.
[6] Williams, *Wilder*, 11.
[7] Sunderland, *Lightning at Hoover's Gap*, 22–24.

Volunteer Infantry, B. F. McGee wrote, "Every fellow seemed to forget his sore feet, his tattered shoes, and all his ills, and go in for a good time. Those that were not drunk laughed themselves almost outside in."[8] On 31 December, they moved toward Munfordville (which may have given Wilder some reservations), and the next day Union scouts reported that General Morgan and his men were giving General Reynolds's Union troops a wide berth. Wilder's men were sent out to intercept General Morgan and his men but were no match on foot in the mud against Morgan's mounted troops. This, no doubt, convinced Wilder of the need to acquire horses for his men.

As horses were not immediately available, Wilder attempted to mount his men of the 17th Indiana on the mules used for the wagon train, but the mules were more interested in getting rid of their riders than pursuing General Morgan. Despite numerous attempts to stay on a mule's back, a would-be rider was quickly bucked off, much to the amusement of members of the 72nd. Thus, they were unsuccessful in their attempt to catch General Morgan and his regiment. The experience with the mules further convinced Wilder of the necessity of getting his men real mounts.

While camping near Cave City, Kentucky, on 2 January 1863, Wilder and his men learned of the Battle of Stones River, which had just ended, near Murfreesboro, Tennessee. Union troops, under command of General Rosecrans, moved toward Bragg's army in Murfreesboro. However, Bragg struck first, sending Generals William J. Hardee and Leonidas Polk to attack Union troops under the command of Major General Alexander M. McCook. Brigadier General Philip Sheridan's troops kept Union forces from giving in and eventually enabled them to hold their ground. Fighting continued for several days,

---

[8] McGee, *History of the 72nd Indiana*, 88.

with losses mounting on both sides. Thinking that more Union forces were on their way, Bragg and his men finally retreated toward nearby Tullahoma.

Wilder and his troops had chased General Morgan into Kentucky, which kept them and, more importantly, General Morgan and his men out of the battle at Stones River, so their efforts had not been entirely in vain. The battle at Stones River had begun on 31 December, and despite high casualties on both sides, there was no clear winner. However, General Bragg would receive criticism from other Confederate officers for his actions during this battle. Several days later Wilder and his men took a fourteen-hour train ride back to Nashville and arrived on the morning of 6 January. Upon arriving in the now Union-held city, they marched through the muddy streets, camping several miles southwest of the city. Their visit was short-lived. With little rest, they were up early the next morning to march thirty miles south to Murfreesboro to join up with Rosecrans's army. Along the way, they saw evidence and aftermath of the Stones River battle.

After the Battle of Stones River, there was a lull in the fighting in Tennessee. General Braxton Bragg brought his Confederate army to an area along the Duck River, between Shelbyville and Wartrace, Tennessee, and set up his headquarters in nearby Tullahoma. General Bragg guarded their position with groups of pickets stationed along a seventy-mile line, which he also hoped would prevent General Rosecrans from moving his Army of the Cumberland to Chattanooga. General Rosecrans kept his troops in Murfreesboro, approximately forty miles away, where they resupplied and trained, despite requests—if not outright orders—from President Lincoln, Secretary of War Edwin Stanton, and General Henry Halleck to attack General Bragg's position. Constant harassment from

General Bragg's cavalry had General Rosecrans requesting more mounted troops instead.[9] On 23 January, Wilder and his brigade, with the 123rd Illinois joining them, traveled to Woodbury, Tennessee, where they had heard seven hundred Confederate cavalry were located. When they arrived, they found that they were too late; other Union troops had already driven them out.[10] In late January, Wilder received an order to combine his command with General James Steedman's 14th Ohio Infantry Regiment. They then traveled to Nashville, arriving on 29 January.

In early February, Colonel Wilder received permission from Rosecrans to proceed with the plan to secure horses for his men. They immediately went foraging in the nearby counties of Dekalb and Wilson, Tennessee, and began accumulating horses.[11] On one occasion during this period, Wilder made his headquarters in a house northeast of Murfreesboro. The lady of the house, evidently pro-Confederate, was indignant over Union troops on her property, as well as having Wilder in her house. Wilder told the woman that they would treat her family as well as pro-Union families in the area were treated.[12]

In a letter to Indiana governor Oliver Morton, dated 9 February, Wilder proudly wrote that the 17th regiment "is in as fine a condition as any regiment in the service. It now numbers nearly six hundred men present. I have got an order from Genl Rosecrans to mount my Brigade." He then added, "my men are highly delighted with their prospects and if no disturbing influence is again thrown in their ranks, will make a

---

[9] Sunderland, *Lightning at Hoover's Gap*, 36.

[10] McManus, Inglis, and Hicks, *Morning to Midnight in the Saddle*, 48.

[11] Ibid., 25–26.

[12] Baumgartner, *Blue Lightning*, 40.

reputation for themselves and add to that of their state."[13] In another letter to Governor Morton, Wilder boasted of constantly harassing General Morgan's men and taking the Confederates' horses for their own use. By doing so, they were able to mount all the men without spending any Union funds.[14]

During the second half of February, the regiment foraged the area for more horses and mules. In a letter to the headquarters of the Inspector General's Office of the Army of the Cumberland, Colonel Joseph C. McKibbin, an aide-de-camp to General George H. Thomas, wrote to Lieutenant Colonel Calvin Goddard of General Rosecrans's staff, that:

> [Wilder's] command presents a fine appearance and will, no doubt, under the command of so efficient and energetic an officer as Col. Wilder, do very good service, in their new capacity. I take this opportunity to make mention of the energy and perseverance with which Col. Wilder is untiringly working to fit out his command, without causing any extra expense to the Government, and would most respectfully ask the Insp. Genl's Office, Department of the Cumberland, to examine the workshops, etc. established by him.[15]

During this time, the regiment was active in building its own wagons, mainly from parts recovered from destroyed wagons, and they shod their own horses.

Wilder's foraging missions around Lebanon and Liberty, Tennessee, were successful. His troops were mostly self-sufficient and employed Black civilians as cooks and workers. The men found food locally, relieving the government of providing rations for them. On one occasion, an enslaved woman

[13] Ibid., 44.

[14] Ibid.

[15] Joseph C. McKibbin to Joseph A. Goddard, 10 March 1863, John T. Wilder Papers, UTC.

approached Wilder and revealed the location of several barrels of salt hidden at her master's home, as well as a cave that hid horses, mules, and weapons. This led to Wilder remarking, "The negroes are our best friends."[16] Once they were fully mounted, the government issued the men cavalry uniforms. So as not to be confused with the regular cavalry, the men tore off the identifying yellow trim from the uniforms.

Wilder's men learned to be self-sufficient and handy. Because every member of Wilder's regiment had a two-foot-long hatchet, they were briefly known as the "Hatchet Brigade." This nickname would be short-lived; soon they would be known by another name. As they moved about, they also created havoc with the Confederates' supply routes by damaging railway lines with a device Wilder created that was referred to as a "rail-twister." By using this device, they effectively rendered a rail line out of commission and damaged it so that it could not be repaired easily or quickly.

Wilder's ability to maintain and enforce discipline on the soldiers was demonstrated on 1 March when a deserter, who had also attempted to kill an officer, was court-martialed. In front of the regiments, the handcuffed prisoner was taken to a large fire. Wilder took a red-hot brand from the fire and burned the letter "D" (for deserter) into his cheek. Then the deserter was led out of the ranks as the band played "The Rogue's March." He was given a blanket, one day's ration, and a canteen of water, and sent away, warning he would be shot if they ever saw him again.[17] In early March they traveled to Woodbury, Tennessee, twenty miles east of Murfreesboro, and again harassed General John Hunt Morgan and his men,

[16] Fitch, *Annals*, 236.

[17] McGee, *History of the 72nd Indiana*, 104.

capturing nearly two dozen soldiers and one officer, with only one of their own wounded.

Idle times for soldiers can often lead to mischief, if not downright rowdiness. In an account by brigade clerk, Henry Tutewiler, Wilder got into a fight with an unruly soldier, a large man who back-talked him. The soldier, after being knocked about some by Wilder, left but then returned with several officers. Unaware as to who Wilder was, the soldier intended to have Wilder arrested. Wilder identified himself and had the officers arrest the soldier.[18]

The 17th Indiana was fully mounted by mid-March 1863, and, by May, Wilder's Brigade would have the only mounted infantry under General Rosecrans's command, with two thousand soldiers on horseback.

Wilder suggested to his wife, Martha, that she travel down to Murfreesboro because he had a "first rate house as a Head Qr's." Captain Eli Lilly (postwar founder of the future pharmaceutical company), who was in the 18th Indiana, was there with his wife and child, and Wilder thought they would provide excellent company for Martha. Murfreesboro, he added, was heavily fortified and safe for her to visit. In a postscript to the letter, he added that he had sent in his resignation the week before, but General Rosecrans had refused it, scolding him first and then complimenting him.[19] At this point, Wilder seems to have grown dissatisfied with the military and even certain superior officers, perhaps due to his success without the formal military training they had received, or his having been abandoned in Munfordville by those who had obtained the proper training in one of the nation's military academies. In a letter to

---

[18] Baumgarter, *Blue Lightning*, 49.

[19] John Wilder to Martha Wilder, 11 March 1863, John T. Wilder Papers, UTC.

Martha on 11 March, Wilder wrote disdainfully of General Charles C. Gilbert, to whom he had appealed to for additional troops and supplies while surrounded by General Bragg's Confederate army at Munfordville, stating that his "conduct at Munfordville, Perryville, and Lebanon, KY, and this last outrageous blunder at Franklin, Tenn. ought to send him to an asylum for Idiots, for a greater Imbecile in uniform does not exist...troops put under Gen. Gilbert are so many men thrown away." Gilbert was criticized by Wilder and others for being too hesitant to act in the battle of Perryville. It is not clear as to what General Gilbert's "blunder" at Franklin, Tennessee, had been as the first of two battles in that town had not yet occurred. Unfortunately, Martha Wilder (or "Pet," as she was known) did not make the trip to Murfreesboro, nor does it appear that she ever traveled to a camp to visit her husband. But with two young children, it may not have been practical. Wilder continued to suffer bouts of dysentery and once had to be brought back to camp in an ambulance while on a scouting trip between Murfreesboro and Franklin.

In mid-March 1863, the 72nd Indiana, which had earlier watched with mirth at the 17th Indiana's first attempts to ride mules, apparently saw the efficacy of using horses and voted in favor of also becoming a mounted regiment. The 75th Indiana voted against it and was reassigned. They were replaced by the 123rd Illinois, which had voted in favor of mounts.

During the first half of 1863, General Bragg's army remained camped near Tullahoma, several dozen miles from Rosecrans's army at Murfreesboro. General Rosecrans continued receiving directives from Washington to attack the Confederates, but resisted doing so, frustrating President Lincoln, Edwin Stanton, and Henry W. Halleck, the commander of all Union armies. This hesitancy was typical of General Rosecrans, who was constantly threatened with being replaced due to his lack of aggressiveness. He was even warned that if he didn't act, he risked having some of his troops sent further south to Vicksburg, Mississippi, to assist General Grant in his move on the city. Rosecrans may have had a good reason not to move on Confederate forces. His Union cavalry was only half of what the Confederates had. Nevertheless, his request for more cavalry was ignored.

In late March, Wilder and his men went out patrolling for eight days and captured 88 prisoners, 460 horses, 8 wagons, 194 slaves, as well as corn and hay from the Confederate troops. They had also engaged Confederate general John A. Wharton's brigade and, according to Wilder, "whipped" them with the loss of two taken as prisoners and one man accidentally killed.[20] He had hoped to capture General Wharton's cavalry, but some of his men, who were to come up from the rear to Wharton's men, took a wrong road. Brigadier General James A. Garfield (the future president) wrote in a report dated 5 April that Wilder had arrived at Carthage, Tennessee, and turned over fifteen prisoners.

In early April, Wilder and his brigade left Murfreesboro and headed west for Franklin, Tennessee, to take part in an attack on Confederate general Earl Van Dorn's Mississippi troops, who were driven away toward Nashville. In late April, the 17th Indiana was moving west of Murfreesboro, into Liberty, Tennessee, where they enjoyed the hospitality of Union-supporting citizens. So grateful was Wilder that he gave money to the children of a family that provided him and his staff dinner. They then went on to Alexandria, Tennessee, about five miles north of Liberty, where they remained for several days and managed to capture several Confederate soldiers, along

---

[20] Ibid., 1 April 1863.

with horses and mules. From there, they advanced on Lebanon. According to Wilder's clerk, Henry Tutewiler, Wilder ordered a small band of soldiers go to the nearby home of Confederate colonel John H. Allison and burn it to the ground. They also scouted around Rome, approximately ten miles east of Lebanon.

After the small affair in Franklin in early April, the combined forces of Wilder's Brigade, Colonel Albert S. Hall's 105th Ohio infantry, and Eli Long's 4th Ohio cavalry journeyed to McMinnville, Tennessee. They were gone for eleven days, traveling fifty miles each day, according to Wilder in a letter to his wife. They destroyed Confederate property and captured more than two hundred prisoners and nearly seven hundred mules and horses.[21] They scattered General John Hunt Morgan's men, burned a cotton factory, and captured a Confederate train, liberating the Union prisoners it carried. However, they did not fulfill Rosecrans's directive to pursue and destroy the Confederate cavalry, and this failure could have been the result of Wilder and General Reynolds not knowing who was in charge, a problem that would surface on occasion.[22]

In May 1863, a revolutionary change in Wilder's Brigade was made, and Wilder played a major part in it, due to strong resources and support he had cultivated prior to the war. Through the first two years of the Civil War, soldiers on both sides had fought with the American Springfield percussion rifles or British Enfield rifles, the standard rifles available at the time. Both of these guns were single-shot arms. Rifles had been used to some good effect in the war and proved better than the muskets used in previous wars. Rifles had better accuracy and longer range, and a practiced marksman could use them to

[21] Ibid., 4 May 1863.

[22] Harbison, "Wilder's Brigade," 21–22.

deadly effect from as far as eight hundred yards. The rifle quickly became the leading weapon in warfare. However, after a single shot, it took time to load them again for another shot, a task complicated by the fact that the loader was probably having to both avoid getting shot by his opponent and keep an eye out for approaching foes bent on capturing or killing him. The act of loading a new bullet into a rifle could take up to a minute with several steps to do in sequence. However, this process was about to change. In 1860 the New Haven Arms Company, which would later become the Winchester Repeating Arms Company, developed the Henry rifle, a sixteen-shot rifle. By 1863, Union troops were using them with positive results, and the demand for the rifles grew. Unfortunately, the New Haven Arms Company could not meet the demands of the Union Army to produce the number requested. In spring 1863, another repeating rifle was marketed, and the company that manufactured these did have the means to meet the demand by the military. Even better, they could offer them at prices significantly cheaper than the Henry rifles. This new gun was the Spencer repeating rifle.

While in Murfreesboro, Tennessee, during spring 1863, Wilder met with a representative of the Spencer Rifle Company, Christopher Miner Spencer, a twenty-seven-year-old machinist and inventor from Connecticut. Wilder had placed an order in March 1863 for nine hundred Henry rifles but could not receive the guns in the time frame he wanted. As a result, he turned to Christopher Spencer, who was in Murfreesboro promoting the Spencer repeating rifle to the Army of the Cumberland. He had patented the gun in 1860 after several years of work. Language in the patent states Spencer's design:

> My invention consists in an improved mode of locking the movable breech of a breechloading firearm, whereby it is

> easily opened and closed, and very firmly secured in place during the explosion of the charge. It also consists in certain contrivances for operating in combination with the movable breech for the purpose of withdrawing the cases of the exploded cartridges from the chamber of the barrel and for conducting new cartridges thereinto from a magazine in the stock.[23]

Spencer patented a newer, improved version in 1862.

Whereas the current single-shot rifles had to be reloaded after each round, the Spencer repeating rifle could get off eight rounds before needing to be reloaded (one in the firing chamber and seven in the loading tube) and created a significant advantage to the soldier using it against a foe with a single-shot rifle. An early field test in 1861 proved that all seven rounds could be fired in just under ten seconds.[24] The Spencer repeating rifle had a lever action and rolling block and featured a loading tube in the stock of the gun, with the bullet being directed into the firing chamber by a lever. Christopher Spencer's father, Ogden Spencer, a manufacturer of wool, originally financed the rifle for a 50 percent share in the profits. By 1861, they had enough investors to form a production company. Christopher Spencer, demonstrating the rifle in Murfreesboro, impressed Wilder with the efficacy of his guns. The company had initially approached the Navy, and in 1861 the rifle was tested by Commander John A. Dahlgren, who was impressed with the gun's capabilities and recommended the Navy conduct further tests. However, the Navy ordered only seven hundred guns, well below the company's hopes. Representatives next approached the Army. General McClellan ordered a test of the rifle and received a favorable review. As a result, the

---

[23] McAulay, *Civil War Breech Loading Rifles*, 93.
[24] Ibid., 95.

Union Army ordered several thousand guns, finally enough for the company to begin mass-producing them. However, the Union Army soon bogged down their orders in red tape and reduction in numbers. The first guns were not delivered until late 1862, and these were divvied out sporadically throughout early 1863.[25]

Even though President Lincoln had personally tried this gun and had been impressed, General James Ripley, the chief ordnance officer for the Union, remained doubtful, so Christopher Spencer worked towards impressing the commanders in the field.[26] General Ripley thought the guns would be too costly and cumbersome because they required special, and larger amounts of, ammunition. Nevertheless, Lincoln had him order ten thousand rifles.[27] Wilder first convinced his men—as if they needed convincing—to purchase these rifles themselves. To assist them, Wilder arranged for funding by procuring money from bankers he knew in his hometown of Greensburg, Indiana. Wilder also contributed funds out of his own pocket. Each member of his regiment signed a promissory note to repay the bank for the $35 gun, their effectiveness certainly worth the expense. However, the federal government stepped in and financed the purchases. With these rifles Wilder would turn his brigade into a much more lethal force than any brigade on either side. His brigade was growing bigger, too. In early May, the 123rd Illinois was reassigned to Wilder's Brigade.

While Wilder was at war, domestic issues at home arose, as they did for other soldiers and officers. Wilder's letters to his wife, "Pet," reveal the child-raising issues, probably normal for

---

[25] Ibid., 97–99.

[26] Sunderland, *Lightning at Hoover's Gap*, 28.

[27] Bruce, *Lincoln and the Tools of War*, 116.

a single parent with several unruly young children, and also contained news and reports of friends and neighbors in the war. In one letter, Wilder expressed disappointment that she had not come to see him at Murfreesboro, and that there had been many wives of the officers there.[28]

On 10 April 1863, their home in Greensburg, Indiana, caught fire. The top of the house was damaged, making it uninhabitable for his wife and children. Wilder attempted to get a pass for ten days to return to Indiana to deal with the situation. Rosecrans denied the request, and Wilder quoted the general in a letter to his wife: "We can't spare you, the Gov[ernmen]t might better build you a dozen houses than to have you away for ten days." Wilder summed this up stating, "So you see the more value one is to the Gov't, the less value he is to himself." Nevertheless, he sent instructions home that unless it were too expensive, she should have the upstairs rebuilt, with the ceiling two feet higher.[29] By early May 1863, Wilder still had not heard from the worker who was to rebuild his home.

His health better for the time being, Wilder remarked in a letter to his wife that he was quite lonesome, without a home to return to. But, he went on, he was glad not to be at home, since the "copperhead" press—the Southern-friendly press in the North—was irritating him with their writings.[30] "I could not stand still and hear my brave companions abused," he wrote, "by the open sympathizers of our common enemy. My blood is too thin, to not run in madness at such traitorous scoundrels." Since his wife was not coming to visit him, he

---

[28] John Wilder to Martha Wilder, 1 April 1863, John T. Wilder Papers, UTC.

[29] Ibid., 16 April 1863.

[30] Copperhead Presses were reporters in the North sympathetic to the Confederates.

added that he had moved out of the house where he had been staying and was now in a tent.[31] Wilder mentioned in a subsequent letter that if they could get their house rebuilt in brick for $1800, then she should go forward with doing it.[32] Wilder also advised his wife to have the title of the house transferred to her name—in case he did not make it home.

Even though his time was monopolized by the war, Wilder also occasionally found time to slip back into his role as industrialist, if not geologist, by collecting and sending some local rock samples home.[33] Minerals and rocks were not the only thing he sent. Wilder also sent home a gift from a man named William McDonald, of Columbus, Ohio: a pair of silver mounted, ivory-handled Navy revolvers in a mahogany case. He wrote that it gave him great pleasure to have something to leave to his children since he had answered the call to arms against the "cowardly ruffians" who were tyrants "practising their brutality on chained slaves, powerless to resist their hated oppressors"; even though Wilder did not espouse racial equality, he neither agreed with nor supported the institution of slavery.[34] Despite the seriousness of the war, Wilder occasionally found time for a little fun. On 9 May, Wilder won $10 from Colonel Henry Jordan in a throwing contest, perhaps by besting his opponent by hurling a rock across Stones River in Tennessee.

---

[31] John Wilder to Martha Wilder, 4 May 1863, John T. Wilder Papers, UTC.

[32] Ibid., 12 May 1863.

[33] Years later, Wilder would have a large personal collection of rocks, fossils, and Indian artifacts; some were passed on to a daughter after his death; others may have been destroyed in a house fire in the early 1900s.

[34] John Wilder to Martha Wilder, 14 June 1863, John T. Wilder Papers, UTC.

On 15 May, the Spencer repeating rifles Wilder ordered arrived. Immediately the men went out to test the new guns, shooting at anything that moved. On 21 May, Wilder's troops were sent out on the Wartrace Road to force back Confederate pickets but were also instructed to avoid a serious engagement. This must have been a disappointment to the men, anxious to use their new rifles in combat for the first time.[35]

In early June, Wilder's Brigade got their first taste of the Spencers' worth and effectiveness in combat. Joined by the Ohio 3rd, 4th, and 10th Regiments, they attacked the 1st Kentucky Cavalry at Lebanon, Tennessee, capturing twenty Confederate soldiers. The following morning, they fought briefly with more Confederate troops, who retreated hastily under the overwhelming fire of the Spencers.[36]

Wilder's health was much better during this period, and his brigade was constantly out foraging or scouting, often skirmishing with Confederates. "We ride into the rebel lines," he wrote his wife, "they firing as we approach, but never waiting to receive a return fire. So far, we have never seen anything but their backs, except when able to cut off their detached command's. They will not fight my command on equal, or double terms."[37] The Confederates were astonished at these new weapons Wilder's men used against them, and before long they were referring to these as "horizontal shot towers." Those Confederates who were captured asked Union soldiers about their "hell-fire guns." Several months after the guns had proven their worth in battles at Hoover's Gap and the bloody battle of Chickamauga, Wilder would also say of the Spencers, "It

[35] Harbison, "Wilder's Brigade," 23–24.

[36] Sunderland, *Lightning at Hoover's Gap*, 34.

[37] John Wilder to Martha Wilder, 14 June 1863, John T. Wilder Papers, UTC.

actually seemed a pity to kill men so. They fell in heaps, and I had it in my heart to order the firing to cease to end the awful sight."[38]

[38] Edwards, *Civil War Guns*, 154.

Chapter 5

Hoover's Gap and the Tullahoma Campaign

Tennessee was important to the Union, and East Tennessee was home to many Union loyalists. President Lincoln hoped to free the state of Confederate control to "free" these loyalists from Confederate rule and possible harassment. Another concern was that the Confederate railroads connecting the western theaters to the eastern theaters, with supplies and troops, ran through Tennessee. President Lincoln was growing frustrated by General Rosecrans's lack of urgency at taking on General Bragg and the Confederate Army of Tennessee. Pressure from Confederate troops attacking supply lines was only one of several reasons Rosecrans had stalled in taking the initiative.[1]

At 4:00 a.m. on 24 June 1863, Wilder's Brigade, made up of the Indiana 17th and the Illinois 123rd, moved out, the first Union troops to head towards Bragg's troops quartered at Shelbyville and Tullahoma, about twenty miles south of Murfreesboro. President Lincoln had been wanting Rosecrans to keep Bragg busy and on guard for fear he would send some of his troops south to Vicksburg, Mississippi, where Union forces under Ulysses S. Grant were besieging Confederates. Rosecrans's advance, with the intent of driving the Confederate forces out of middle Tennessee, would become known as the Tullahoma Campaign. Wilder's Brigade was chosen by General William S. Rosecrans to lead the first Union troops.

Several hours after Wilder's troops departed, the Union regiments of Generals Reynolds, Rousseau, and Negley's divisions also began their advance. In front of them was a long

---

[1] Harbison, "Wilder's Brigade," 3.

ridge, broken by three gaps, which were defended by the troops of Confederate generals Leonidas Polk, William J. Hardee, and Alexander P. Stewart. General Rosecrans was intending to take Hoover's Gap, eleven miles south of Murfreesboro, and the eastern-most of the three gaps, after making a feint on the other two gaps to draw more Confederate troops in that direction.[2]

After months of inactivity around Tullahoma, Bragg's Confederate troops were finally forced into action by Rosecrans's bringing the fight to them. As Wilder's men moved through the early summer rain, they looked forward to a battle with Confederate troops, if only to see just what their new Spencer rifles could do. At 10:00 a.m., six hours after starting, Wilder's Brigade arrived at Hoover's Gap, a full nine miles ahead of the other Union troops. Their objective was to hold their position, and the gap, until General Reynolds's infantry arrived. By this time, Wilder's troops had been joined by the 72nd Indiana, the 98th Illinois, and Captain Eli Lilly's 18th Indiana.

General Bragg had placed troops along the gaps in the hills in an attempt to stop or at least slow Union troops. Arriving at Hoover's Gap at full gallop, Wilder's Brigade surprised pickets from the Confederate 1st Kentucky cavalry, the same soldiers they had skirmished with three weeks earlier. Wilder's Brigade drove them back into a hill covered with cedars, where the Rebels were joined by other Confederate pickets. The remainder of the 1st Kentucky Cavalry, having met Wilder's men head on, were quickly driven back in such haste that they left their battle flag. The 1st Kentucky Cavalry was quickly reinforced by Confederate brigades from Georgia, Alabama, and Tennessee, under commands of Generals William Bate and Bushrod Johnson. The Spencer rifles were so effective that General Bate had

---

[2] Hicken, *Illinois in the Civil War*, 190.

at first thought his troops were vastly outnumbered.[3] The Union forces captured two of the Confederate pickets while suffering no casualties. Wilder was then emboldened to take the gap, even though he knew that a Confederate Kentucky cavalry was only one mile ahead, as well as other Confederate infantry in the vicinity. Determined to take and hold Hoover's Gap, a confident Wilder charged ahead.

So effective was their charge that they were able to advance much farther than they had intended. In fact, they were so far ahead they were cut off from the rest of the Union brigades and were now facing two Tennessee brigades. Wilder placed two companies of the 98th Illinois on one side of the gap and four companies of the Indiana 17th a quarter mile away on a hill dense with trees. He further fortified the area with men both for observation and to prevent Confederate troops from advancing in the area. John N. King, of the 92nd Illinois, wrote in his journal, "Colonel Wilder's mounted infantry could not be driven an inch from a front charge, no matter how quick the rebels came."[4]

Confederate general Alexander P. Stewart's troops, who were part of General Hardee's Corps of the Army of Tennessee, had been advancing on the site and were now closing in. Wilder's men heard their movement and dug in their positions at the south end of Hoover's Gap. Captain Eli Lilly placed two Howitzers in front of the Indiana 72nd, and four Rodman 10-pound guns on a hill facing the direction of Stewart's incoming troops. For support, soldiers from the 123rd Illinois were placed nearby on both sides of Lilly's battery. The 123rd Illinois was a young regiment, organized the year before, and had cut their teeth in the Battle of Perryville in early October 1862.

---

[3] Williams, *Wilder*, 19.

[4] Swedberg, ed., *Three Years with the 92nd Illinois*, 97.

Although the Union troops were physically fatigued from the long march (their horses gave out several miles back, which forced the men to drag the artillery through mud for over a mile), they were still eager to see what their Spencer rifles could do to the advancing Confederate troops.

General Bate had positioned two Tennessee brigades to his right and an Alabama brigade to his left. Once in place, his men began their advance. The Confederate soldiers poured from the woods, emitting their "rebel yell." Lilly's cannons responded, opening fire on them from their advantageous position on a hill. Shooting back furiously, the Confederates were able at first to continue their advance. Armed with mostly smooth-bore muzzle loaders, the Confederate soldiers then faced the hail of bullets from the Spencer rifles of the 123rd Illinois, who rose from their positions and opened fire in a lethal fusillade. The Confederates were first stopped in their tracks as many fell, but they quickly regrouped and attempted another advance. They soon realized, however, that they were in a futile situation and retreated, unable to counter the Union fighters and their Spencer rifles. After this, the artillery guns on both sides continued firing at each other.

General Bate sent four brigades to attack the 17th Indiana, and these faced the Spencer rifles as well. The Confederates were able to replace fallen soldiers quickly, and despite the heavy fire they drew, they made a slow advance to within fifty feet of the 17th Indiana before falling back. Some of the Union soldiers had fired their rifles so many times that they had exhausted their ammunition, so the Confederate forces were able to begin another advance. Wilder sent the 98th Illinois, led by Colonel Funkhouser, over to support the 17th. Together the 17th Indiana and the 98th Illinois overwhelmed the

Confederate troops, some getting as close as twenty yards, and then charged down towards them, sending them retreating in panic.

Undeterred, Generals Bate and Johnson again organized the Confederate troops for another attack on Wilder's men. General Reynolds's adjutant was sent to Wilder with instructions to withdraw. Even though he was facing General Stewart's entire division, Wilder felt his men could hold their ground, and refused the order. After Wilder's refusal to withdraw, Bate's and Johnson's brigades attacked Wilder's men, but his troops did as Wilder said they would—they held their ground and repulsed the Confederate troops.[5]

Wilder's weary troops were soon reinforced by the 21st Indiana Battery, which allowed Wilder's men a chance for some much-needed rest. Wilder would later write a colleague about the Spencer rifles,

> My Brigade of Mounted Infantry have repeatedly routed and driven largely superior forces of rebels, in some instances five or six times our number and this result is mainly due to our being armed with the Spencer repeating rifle. Since using this gun we have never been driven a single rod by any kind of force or number of the enemy. At Hoover's Gap, in Tennessee, on June 24, 1863, one of my regiments fairly defeated a rebel brigade of five regiments, they admitting a loss of over 500, whilst our loss was 47. No line of men, who come within fifty yards of another force armed with Spencer repeating rifles, can either get away alive, or reach them with a charge, as in either case they are certain to be destroyed by the terrible fire poured into their ranks by cool men thus armed. My men feel as if it is impossible

---

[5] Later, as he explained his insubordination, General Rosecrans told General Reynolds that Wilder had made the correct decision and was to be promoted then.

> to be whipped, and the confidence inspired by these arms added to their terribly destructive capacity, fully quadruples the effectiveness of my command.[6]

During the battle, the Union troops lost only one officer, Lieutenant J. Moreland of the 17th Indiana. Twelve enlisted men were killed, with forty-seven wounded. Confederate losses were twenty-one killed and 129 wounded. After the battle, General George H. Thomas would tell Wilder personally, "You have saved the lives of a thousand men by your gallant conduct today. I didn't expect to get the gap for three days."[7] Despite the praise, some were not as impressed with Wilder and his actions at Hoover's Gap. Reynolds was growing impatient with Wilder, who often went around him in the chain of command.[8]

On 27 June, Wilder received orders from General Rosecrans via Joseph J. Reynolds to chase and harass Confederate troops who were traveling south. When they arrived at Winchester Pike, they found that the Confederates had retreated toward Fairfield, Tennessee. Wilder's men camped six miles from Manchester, and the next morning moved into the town, capturing forty Confederates, including one captain and three lieutenants. When General Reynolds arrived, Wilder sent Captain Lawson S. Kilbourn with members of the 17th Indiana to destroy the train tracks of the McMinnville Railroad several miles from Tullahoma. The next day they moved into Tullahoma, destroying Confederate communication lines. Heading directly east they next traveled twenty miles to Hillsboro, leaving two companies of the 123rd Illinois there and then headed for Decherd to the southwest. Coming to the Elk

---

[6] Edwards, *Civil War Guns,* 149–50.

[7] Connolly, *Three Years in the Army of the Cumberland,* 94.

[8] Harbison, "Wilder's Brigade," 41–42.

River, they discovered the river too swollen to cross safely and went up to the town of Pelham, where they knew a bridge spanned the river. As they approached Pelham, they learned that a small team of Confederates was there and intent on destroying the bridge. Wilder sent a group of soldiers under the command of Lieutenant Colonel Edward Kitchell of the 98th Illinois to prevent the Confederates from damaging the bridge. This they did and captured two Confederates and a team of seventy-eight mules. While at Pelham they also burned a saddle factory.

When Wilder and his men arrived back at the Elk River, they swam the horses across and built a raft to ferry their Howitzers over. Once they had crossed the river, they set their sights on Decherd and arrived there at 8 p.m., at which point they engaged a small band of Confederates protecting their garrison and railroad. They prevented Wilder's men from doing much damage, but Wilder's troops eventually drove these Confederates out and began destroying the rail lines that connected Nashville and Chattanooga. On 30 June, Wilder learned from several prisoners that a large Confederate force was heading their way. Wilder was certainly not eager to repeat his Munfordville experience, so, rather than face a large army, they vacated the area. General Nathan Bedford Forrest was part of this oncoming force and intended to capture Wilder at Pelham, about fifteen miles northeast of Decherd.

As this activity was happening in Tennessee, two other major battles of the war were ongoing. One was far up north, in Gettysburg, Pennsylvania, and the other was in the South, at Vicksburg, Mississippi, which had been under siege by Union troops for nearly a year. In both battles the Union army was victorious, sending a crippling blow to the power and morale of the Confederate army and the Confederate states. With the victory at Vicksburg, Union forces led by General U. S. Grant now controlled the Mississippi River, and in the north, Union forces under General George Meade had defeated Confederate troops led by Robert E. Lee.

On 1 July, Wilder and his men headed up Cumberland Mountain, and the next morning they could see a large Confederate force nearing Dechard. Wilder's troops were moving towards Sewanee, home of the recently established University of the South, and destroyed the Tracy City railroad line along the way. Wilder then commanded Colonel John J. Funkhouser, of the 98th Illinois, to take 450 men and do the same to the railway at Tantallon. He then proceeded to Anderson, on the Tennessee/Alabama border, to destroy the railway there, but upon discovering that the area was guarded by Confederate troops (made up from General Simon Bolivar Buckner's men), they decided against the destruction. Instead, Wilder gathered his troops and started down Cumberland Mountain.

It was raining heavily, and because of the rain gear both sides were wearing, it was hard to distinguish Union soldiers and officers from their Confederate counterparts. It was so difficult, in fact, that General Forrest, chasing after Wilder, soon found himself face to face with Union troops, who were unaware that he was a Confederate, or who he was. Realizing the situation, Forrest pretended to be part of a Union cavalry and allowed the Union troops to pass by. Then he positioned his men alongside the road, under cover, to wait the retreat of the Union troops as they encountered a larger Confederate force Forrest knew was coming. However, just as they were getting set, Forrest observed Wilder's main force coming up along the road behind the first Union force. He quickly directed his men back but didn't get far before running into the Union force that had first passed them. Now they had realized who he was.

There was a brief skirmish. General Forrest's troops killed and captured several Union soldiers, creating chaos among the Union troops. General Forrest then set his sights on capturing Wilder, but by this time Wilder had managed to escape.[9]

Wilder and his men then headed first for Manchester, and then Pelham, riding hard for several days. They eventually ended up at Normandy, between Manchester and Shelbyville, for several days of much-needed rest and foraging. Through several battles and skirmishes, Wilder's men had shown how effective and lethal the Spencer rifles were. Impressed with their new fighting weapon, General George H. Thomas declared that Wilder's Brigade, until then known as the Hatchet Brigade, would now be known as the Lightning Brigade.[10]

Battle-weary and drained of ammunition and equipment, General Rosecrans rested his Army of the Cumberland near Tullahoma. Wilder's Lightning Brigade camped at Normandy, seven miles northwest of Rosecrans. Meanwhile, General Braxton Bragg had moved his Confederate army south to Chattanooga, on the Tennessee/Georgia state line. Wilder again suffered through another bout with dysentery, this time during an inactive period, fortunately.

During six weeks of the early summer, the Army of the Cumberland would replenish its supplies, including horses and mules foraged from nearby Decherd and Wartrace. The area farms, gardens, and orchards provided good sources of food. News of the recent Union victories at Gettysburg and Vicksburg reached them and no doubt lifted their spirits. On 8 July, they were joined by the 92nd Illinois, commanded by Colonel Smith Atkins. Two days earlier, Wilder had observed the 92nd

---

[9] Williams, *Wilder*, 21–22.

[10] Sunderland, *Lightning at Hoover's Gap*, 49–53.

working on a bridge and had been impressed enough with them to request having them added to his brigade.

On 12 July, the Lightning Brigade set off on a seven-day foraging mission. They found the Tennessee towns of Shelbyville and Farmington to be Union-friendly, so they camped at Farmington. The next day they rode into the pro-Confederate town of Lewisburg, only five miles from Farmington, liberated Union sympathizers from the jail before burning it, and raided the stores for supplies. From there they went to Columbia, fifteen miles northwest, and captured three Confederate officers and thirty soldiers. More mobile now that they had horses, they next traveled thirty miles northwest to Centerville, capturing more Confederate soldiers and horses. They finished the expedition by traveling eighty miles east to Normandy, with several brigades taking a side trip to destroy saltpeter works at Lynchburg, which was supplying necessary gunpowder ingredients for Confederate troops.

On 21 July, Wilder took leave, possibly health-related or to check on progress of his house restoration, and went home to Indiana for a short visit. While he was gone, Colonel A. O. Miller was placed in command. The Lightning Brigade remained at Normandy until late July and then relocated twenty miles to Decherd, where they remained mostly inactive for several weeks. They spent their time foraging for fresh horses and mules, something General Joseph J. Reynolds saw as unsanctioned. During Wilder's absence, Reynolds issued several reprimands to the brigade for their foraging as it appears that some within the brigade were taking liberties with the locals, helping themselves to liquor and other household items in violation of approved military policy regarding foraging. Perhaps Reynolds was jealous of Wilder's rising status within the ranks, but he was concerned about Wilder's going around him in communicating with his other superiors.[11]

Colonel John T. Wilder and his Lightning Brigade were quickly becoming the talk of the Union forces in the western theater of the Civil War, and soldiers throughout the Union Army now wanted both horses and Spencer repeating rifles. Men were willing to re-enlist only if they had a mount and a Spencer rifle. President Lincoln was in favor of supplying troops with mounts and repeating rifles, but Secretary of War Edwin Stanton and General-in-Chief Henry Halleck did not share the president's eagerness, perhaps due to frustration with General Rosecrans and his reluctance to march on Bragg in Chattanooga.[12] Despite President Lincoln's request that General Rosecrans launch an offensive against General Bragg's army in Chattanooga, General Rosecrans yet again demurred, feeling that he needed additional soldiers and supplies to launch a successful campaign.

On 16 August, the Army of the Cumberland finally set forth for Chattanooga and Bragg's army. Wilder's Lightning Brigade, with Wilder back from Indiana and again in command, left Decherd and rode in the rain to the top of Cumberland Mountain, passing by the University of the South in Sewanee. The Lightning Brigade, for the march to Chattanooga, had been assigned to General Thomas L. Crittenden's corps and was to give the false impression that the Union Army was crossing the Tennessee River north of Chattanooga. On 19 August, they were in the Sequatchie Valley, north of Chattanooga, where food and game were plentiful. Unfortunately, so were Confederate pickets.

---

[11] Harbison, "Wilder's Brigade," 48–49.

[12] Ibid., 51–54.

The 92nd Illinois became so mired down dealing with the Confederate sharpshooters that an exasperated Wilder sent in the 72nd Indiana to support them. After giving chase to the pickets, killing and capturing some, they finally eliminated the resistance. That evening, Wilder sent four companies of his 17th Indiana into the small town of Jasper where they killed one Confederate soldier, wounded another, and captured eight.[13] The next day they worked their way up and over Walden's Ridge, a long narrow mountain only a few miles outside of Chattanooga. Wilder had loaded mules with provisions so they would not have to pull their wagons up the steep mountain. That night they rested at Poe's Tavern, north of Chattanooga near the towns of Soddy and Daisy.

On 21 August, Wilder directed the 92nd Illinois, along with Eli Lilly's 18th Indiana, to head for Chattanooga and Harrison's Landing, directly north of the town, for the purpose of drawing more attention north of Chattanooga. This ploy, however, would be canceled by General John M. Palmer, of the 14th Corps of the Army of the Cumberland, when he learned of the high number of Confederate troops and sharpshooters in that area. Nonetheless, Wilder's men were still able to capture twelve Confederates and several dozen mules. The Union forces moved south to Stringer's Ridge, just across the Tennessee River from Chattanooga, to join other Union troops. On 25 August, Wilder captured three Confederate deserters. They reported, erroneously, that General Bragg had retreated to Atlanta when in truth he was just south of Chattanooga. This information likely confused Rosecrans.[14]

From the higher vantage point of Stringer's Ridge, Union forces announced their arrival by firing cannons across the river

[13] Swedberg, ed., *Three Years with the 92nd Illinois*, 105.

[14] Harbison, "Wilder's Brigade," 56.

toward downtown Chattanooga. Newspaper reporter Henry Watterson, who was working on the *Chattanooga Rebel*, a Confederate newspaper, was in the Presbyterian church with his fiancée when the shelling began. Although it wasn't a Sunday, many citizens were in church as President Jefferson Davis had called for a day of prayer. In the middle of a prayer, a cannonball tore the steeple off the church, sending most of the congregation to the exits in search of better shelter.

Halfway down Stringer's Ridge was a small frame house; Wilder and several officers decided to walk to it to get a better look across the river. Thinking they were moving unobserved by Confederate forces across the river, they entered the house, and, using field glasses, attempted to observe action on the Confederate side in Chattanooga. The Confederates, well aware of their presence, immediately shot a cannonball at the house. It hit under the elevated porch, killing a large sow and sending mud, wood, and parts of the pig everywhere. Wilder and the officers scrambled from the house and got up the hill most certainly faster than they had come down.[15] The Union forces stayed on their side of the river and shelled Chattanooga for several days. They sank several riverboats on the river, destroyed a few Confederate guns, and lost one artilleryman. At night, Wilder had his men spread out across the river and build many campfires to give the impression there were larger in number than they really were.[16] President Lincoln and General Halleck would finally get their wish, as Rosecrans's army was finally going to take on General Bragg's Confederate forces.

---

[15] McGee, *History of the 72nd Indiana*, 147–48.

[16] Harbison, "Wilder's Brigade," 55.

Chapter 6

The Battle of Chickamauga

General Rosecrans's Army of the Cumberland began crossing the Tennessee River, south of Chattanooga, on 2 September while the Confederates were expecting them to cross the wide river north of the city. In fact, Wilder and his men had been sent north of Chattanooga to do just that and to draw attention away from south of Chattanooga, but the plan was eventually cancelled after the Confederates sent an army corps to prevent them from crossing. As a result, the Army of the Cumberland crossed south of Chattanooga mostly undetected. After the crossing, Union troops stationed themselves on either side of the city, extending as far down as Georgia. On 9 September, when General Bragg realized that the Union army was south of him, he concocted a plan in which to trap them. He would fake a retreat to Atlanta but fall back only a few miles south into north Georgia, then turn to meet the pursuing Union forces head on. By then, he hoped to have received additional troops and have a fighting force equal to the Union Army. Furthermore, the flatter terrain would be better suited to engage them in battle. To help with this plan, General Bragg arranged for several soldiers to get captured and give reports that the Confederate Army was completely demoralized and in disarray, in hopes of causing the Union army to drop its guard a bit. Also on the ninth, Wilder and his brigade finally received orders to cross the Tennessee River and move into Chattanooga, a move that took a full two days to complete. With no Confederate forces left in the city, they and other Union troops entered Chattanooga with no resistance.

On 10 September, soldiers from the 123rd Illinois who were five miles east of Chattanooga at Tyner's Station came into possession of a bag of Confederate mail. In this mail bag was information of General Bragg's intentions and movements, leading Wilder to report that Bragg was moving his troops further south to Rome, Georgia. Unfortunately, this was not the case as Bragg and his forces were gathering near Lee and Gordon's Mills, around the community of Chickamauga, Georgia.[1]

General Rosecrans's troops split into three columns while in pursuit of the "retreating" Confederates, despite being warned against doing so by General George H. Thomas. Rosecrans's pursuit gave the advantage to General Bragg, who could attack each column separately, exactly as Bragg had hoped. Union general Crittenden began moving toward Lee and Gordon's Mill in Chickamauga.

Union general James S. Negley's troops were in a spot advantageous for General Bragg to attack him, and Bragg directed two of his generals to make the attack. However, Bragg no longer had the respect of many of his subordinates, including General Leonidas Polk, who ignored the directive, which allowed General Negley and his men to escape. General Rosecrans, still believing the Confederate Army was retreating and completely demoralized, pressed on although not quite sure of Bragg's whereabouts. The Lightning Brigade moved south to Ringgold, Georgia, on 11 September, running into soldiers from Forrest's cavalry. Getting some reinforcements, they drove the Confederates back south of Ringgold. Wilder's men continued to chase them until ordered back the next day to Ringgold.

---

[1] Harbison, "Wilder's Brigade," 58–59.

Also on 12 September, General Rosecrans ordered General Alexander McCook and his cavalry to join up with General Thomas at Stevens Gap in northwest Georgia, as they moved to join General Crittenden at Ringgold, approximately fifteen miles south of Chattanooga. Wilder and his men were also at Ringgold, and they received orders to report to General Joseph J. Reynolds's division at LaFayette, Georgia, a short distance from Ringgold. As they marched, they encountered Confederate troops and pickets, engaged them in brief skirmishes, and drove them south toward Dalton, Georgia. During this time, a rumor circulated that Wilder and his men had been captured, a rumor that even General Rosecrans briefly believed.[2]

The next day, 13 September, General Bragg ordered General Leonidas Polk to attack General Crittenden's 21st Corps, now at Lee and Gordon's Mill on West Chickamauga Creek. Polk again ignored Bragg's order. While Bragg's officers mostly ignored his orders, Rosecrans was able to gather and strengthen his army over the following several days.

By 17 September, Bragg had decided to advance his army northward, moving back toward Chattanooga. This move, he thought, would force Rosecrans to either attack or withdraw. Rosecrans directed the Lightning Brigade to Alexander's Bridge to defend the bridge and report on Confederate troop movements. On 18 September, Confederate general Bushrod Johnson's men met pickets from Union general Robert Minty's brigade, which was guarding Reed's Bridge. Outnumbered, Minty's men withdrew across the bridge, unable to destroy it, which gave open access for General Johnson's men to cross. South of this, Wilder's Lightning Brigade, although outnumbered, successfully guarded Alexander's Bridge with their Spencer rifles and Eli Lilly's cannons.

---

[2] McGee, *History of the 72nd Indiana*, 162.

By now, the two armies were on opposite sides of West Chickamauga Creek, near Lee and Gordon's Mill, skirmishing against each other. General Bragg continued moving his troops to the north, placing them between the Union troops and Chattanooga, now in hopes of forcing the Union troops southward to the mountains, where he believed they would be more vulnerable and where he could destroy them. The Union troops at Reed's and Alexander's Bridges were able to slow the advancing Confederate troops. Before the end of the day, Wilder had his men pull up planks on the bridge to prevent Confederate wagons from crossing. Because of the Lightning Brigade's defense, General Rosecrans, on the evening of 18 September, was able to move his troops to more strategic positions. That evening, Wilder sought out and consulted with General Thomas, who directed Wilder to move his brigade to the West Viniard Field. As a result, on the morning of 19 September, Wilder found his troops in the center, instead of the extreme left. He and his men were now between the Union troops of General Horatio Van Cleve and General Jefferson C. Davis, west of the Chattanooga-Lafayette Road. As the morning broke, Thomas's men joined the Lightning Brigade, which was in a line along a fence, in front of a thickly wooded area but facing an open field. The battle of Chickamauga thus began the morning of 19 September, near Alexander's Bridge, with General Absalom Baird's divisions fighting Forrest's Cavalry.

Confederate General James Longstreet succeeded in getting reassigned to the western theater after the July loss at Gettysburg and arrived after a nine-day train trip from Virginia. General Bragg immediately assigned Longstreet one of the two wings of Confederate forces, sending Longstreet to unfamiliar territory. General Bragg assigned command of the other wing to General Polk. Around noon, the battle had moved toward the Lightning Brigade, which had enough Spencer rifles and ammunition to shoot 160,000 rounds. The Lightning Brigade soon found themselves supporting both Davis's and Van Cleve's Divisions, although they were half a mile apart. In a letter home to his wife, Otho James McManus, a member of the 123rd Illinois, wrote,

> Col. Wilder ordered us to make our position as strong as possible and before an hour, we had built a pretty fair breast-work nearly half a mile long, behind which we and Spencers were ready for all the lines that rebs could against us.... But they did not come up to our part of the line of battle.... Along our left where the fighting was going on heaviest, the rebs seemed to get the better of Sheridan's Division about twelve or one o'clock when he [Sheridan] sent to Wilder asking if he [Wilder] could help him.[3]

At approximately noon, Wilder's men were attacked by Confederate forces advancing toward Alexander's Bridge. Wilder and his men had been assigned to a position several hundred yards from General Rosecrans's headquarters. He also had two well-armed regiments and two artillery sections along Chickamauga Creek to defend the bridge. Eli Lilly's men of the 18th Indiana were four hundred yards away, near the Alexander House. Learning that General Minty was under attack and knowing he would be outflanked if Minty withdrew, Wilder sent reinforcements for Minty's men. Sixteen thousand Confederate troops, led by Generals Forrest, Walker, and Johnson, attacked Wilder and Minty's troops, which numbered only fifteen hundred. Lilly's battery opened up on the Confederate forces as they approached Wilder's men, firing

[3] McManus, Inglis, and Hicks, *Morning to Midnight in the Saddle*, 114.

percussion and long-range shells at the Confederates. Forrest's men returned fire. General John Bell Hood's men, with members of General Jerome B. Robertson's brigade, attacked General Jefferson C. Davis's men, driving them back in a confused panic. Wilder ordered Colonels James Monroe and A. O. Miller, with the 123rd Illinois and the 72nd Indiana, to move right and attack the Confederates, which they did, driving the Confederates back.

As both Union and Confederate forces fought to what was amounting to a stalemate, Confederate general A. P. Stewart sent General Bate's men in, who were held in check by the Lightning Brigade. Wilder gave orders to the 98th Illinois and the 17th Indiana to attack Stewart's left flank, and, with two of Lilly's artillery guns, they forced the Confederates into a retreat. They then held off two units of Confederates, led by Generals Evander McNair and John Gregg, with a furious attack from both their Spencer rifles and Lilly's guns. At this point Wilder sent his men to support General Davis in the West Viniard Field.

At four o'clock in the afternoon, Wilder received word that General Minty had abandoned the bridge he was defending. Wilder's men destroyed the Alexander's Bridge and then moved nearby to the Viniard House. Once there, Wilder reported to a dubious General Thomas L. Crittenden that Confederate troops were approaching. The army that was advancing on them was General Hood's corps, which included General Bushrod Johnson's men. It wasn't until General Minty arrived and gave a similar report that Crittenden readied his men for battle. Crittenden then looked at Wilder and told him he expected a good report from him. Crittenden moved his infantry forward, but they soon came under heavy fire, causing them to retreat in a panic, running past Wilder and Minty's men. "The General has his report," yelled Wilder to Minty, loud enough for General Crittenden to hear.

Confederate troops, commanded by General Hood, approached within thirty yards of Wilder's men, who then opened up with their Spencer rifles, causing the Confederates to fall back. A second attack was also repulsed. Wilder's men continued to hold their position for several more hours. During this time, Rosecrans moved General George H. Thomas and his troops northward to block the Confederate advance.

Union general Philip Sheridan and his troops arrived on the scene to bold cries of "make way for Sheridan!" by a staff officer carrying Sheridan's battle flag. Sheridan's troops then passed through Wilder's men, who opened their ranks to let them pass. Sheridan's men then stormed the woods, only to find it full of Confederates who greeted them with a furious onslaught, sending Sheridan's men scrambling back out of the woods with the Confederates giving chase. They ran back through Wilder's men, who could not resist shouting derisively "make way for Sheridan!" The Confederates, remembering their earlier meeting with the Spencer rifles, did not advance on Wilder's men.

Confederate sharpshooters had taken position behind a cabin several hundred yards in front of the Lightning Brigade. At dusk, the Confederates charged, screaming their notorious rebel yell. The Lightning Brigade opened up with their Spencers, decimating the Confederate lines. Captain Eli Lilly arranged his cannons to fire into the ditch where the Confederate soldiers who were not yet wounded or killed had taken refuge. So effective were his cannons, and perhaps in sympathy to the Confederate soldiers on the receiving end, that Captain Lilly eventually gave the command to cease fire after many had been killed. By this time night had fallen. Wilder's Brigade suffered five killed and fifteen wounded. Unable to get to the wounded still in the fields for fears of snipers, both sides had to endure a night of hearing the heart-rending cries of the wounded calling out for help.

Due to General Polk failing to give orders to Hill's troops, who were to resume fighting by attacking General Thomas's men, the battle on 20 September didn't begin as General Bragg intended. Bragg ordered all the division commanders into action, with small skirmishes erupting. Neither side gained an advantage after several hours of fighting. By mid-morning a gap was believed to have opened up in the Union lines. Union general Thomas J. Wood, who knew there was no gap, was ordered by General Rosecrans to move his troops to this supposed gap. Having had a run-in with General Rosecrans shortly before, Wood followed the order despite knowing he was *creating* a gap by leaving his area. Confederate General Longstreet took advantage of this move and had his men attack the Union right side. His men moved through the new gap with ease, creating chaos with the Union troops and sending many in retreat toward Chattanooga, General Rosecrans included. General Thomas and his men were then in danger of being overtaken.

Around mid-day on this second day of battle, General McCook ordered Wilder to close the line on the right, as he, McCook, was moving to the left. The Lightning Brigade moved up the small hill at the Widow Glenn's house. General Sheridan's brigade was attacked by Confederate general Thomas C. Hindman's men, who drove the 27th Illinois off, briefly capturing the battery. Wilder then ordered Colonel Funkhauser to storm the position, which they did, retaking the battery.

Wilder's soldiers were joined at the Widow Glenn's house by the 39th Indiana, led by Colonel T. J. Harrison. With these additional troops, Wilder led a charge that was immediately met by several lines of Confederates scarcely fifty yards in front of them, bayonets leveled and screaming rebel yells. The Union troops shot continuously into them with their Spencer rifles, eventually thinning their ranks and driving them back. Wilder ordered a halt in the firing, and the Confederate troops, led by General Arthur M. Manigault, regrouped and again advanced, despite being severely reduced in number. Once more they received heavy fire from the Union troops and retreated. Several more times they attempted an advance, but Wilder's troops held them back with their Spencer rifles. Wilder gave the order to pursue them, and they drove Manigault's men back nearly a mile. During this time, Confederate troops under General Hindman were advancing on Wilder's left and rear. They engaged in a short fight near a small pond that would become known as "Bloody Pond" from the wounded soldiers who were trying to get water from it.

The Lightning Brigade was the only Union brigade remaining on the Union right, and it was holding its position. Knowing that General Thomas needed assistance, Wilder had the Lightning Brigade charge through Hindman and Johnson's divisions to join Thomas, despite being heavily outnumbered. However, the Spencer rifles made up for the difference. Wilder sent a message to General Sheridan, who was on retreat to Chattanooga, to join him, which Sheridan declined. Wilder gave his men a brief respite to get water, and they did so amidst the carnage surrounding Bloody Pond. Wilder's Lightning Brigade then came to Thomas's rescue, attacking Longstreet's flank, stopping its advance. Other Union troops from various regiments reinforced Thomas's right and rear positions. They were joined by General Gordon Granger's reserve corps, and together these Union forces protected General Thomas and his men.

Wilder directed his brigade to charge forward, leaving a gap for Eli Lilly's artillery. Shortly after their advance began, Charles Dana, the assistant secretary of war, rode up and, misinformed, told Colonel Wilder that the Union Army had been annihilated, that General Rosecrans had been killed, and that Wilder was to escort him back to Chattanooga. Wilder, knowing better, told Secretary Dana that General Thomas was still holding his position at Snodgrass Hill and that the situation was not as dire as he had reported. But Dana persisted, continuing to ask Wilder for escort to Chattanooga. Wilder had no interest in taking Dana to Chattanooga (even though Dana could have ordered him to do so) but ended his attack and headed for an area known as McFarland's Gap.[4] Confederate forces attempted to break this line throughout the day but failed, earning General George H. Thomas the now well-known nickname "Rock of Chickamauga." Because of General Thomas's stand, Union forces were able to retreat that night, first to Rossville, Georgia, and then north to Chattanooga. General Thomas, upon hearing Wilder's Brigade was still intact, ordered them to shore up his right side against a Confederate charge. Wilder did so, and they remained there until the next morning. Then they were given the order to withdraw, the last Union regiment to leave the Chickamauga battlefield. Wilder and his Lightning Brigade so delayed Braxton Bragg's army from attacking General Thomas that Thomas was able to properly prepare for the eventual Confederate attack and make a stand at Snodgrass Hill. General Thomas would later tell

[4] Wilder's accounts of this incident would change over the years and conflict slightly with Dana's account, which claims Wilder asked him for orders.

Wilder that he and his Spencer-equipped soldiers no-doubt saved the Union forces from total destruction during this battle, as he had also done earlier at Alexander's Bridge. Two months later General Thomas would recommend Wilder for promotion to brigadier general:

Headquarters

Department of the Cumberland
Chattanooga, November 27, 1863

Brigadier-General Lorenze Thomas,
Adjutant—General, U.S. Army

General: Enclosed herewith I have the honor to transmit the report of Col. John T. Wilder, Seventeenth Indiana Volunteers, commanding Brigade of mounted infantry, of the Cumberland before and after the evacuation of Chattanooga by the rebel army, including the battle of Chickamauga, and up to the time of the assembling of the army at Chattanooga.

For his ingenuity and fertility of resource in occupying the attention of the entire corps of the rebel army while our army was getting around its flank, and for his valor and the many qualities of a commander displayed by him in the numerous engagements of his Brigade with the enemy before and during the battle of Chickamauga, and for the excellent service rendered by him generally, I would respectfully recommend him to the President of the United States for an appointment of Brigadier General.

I am sir, very respectfully, your obedient servant,

George H. Thomas
Major-General, Commanding.

The battle at Chickamauga would be one of the bloodiest battles during the Civil War. An estimated 125,000 soldiers had fought in the two-day battle. Over 4,000 soldiers were killed, with a total number of casualties—killed, wounded, or captured and missing—well over 34,000.[5]

On 24 September, exhausted and again sick, Wilder went home to Indiana.[6] Several months resting back home in Greensburg, Indiana, seemed the best remedy. Wilder had been active the better part of the year in General Rosecrans's Tullahoma Campaign and had just survived a major battle at Chickamauga. The regimental doctor, Dr. Samuel E. Munford, wrote in a letter dated 22 September that Wilder had typhoid malarial fever, with inflammation of the stomach, and had, in the past three months, lost thirty pounds.[7] How Colonel John Wilder was able to perform his duties in this condition, particularly during the Chickamauga battle, is hard to imagine. But he did, and afterward, went home to recover his health and strength.

During his recovery at home in Indiana in fall 1863, Wilder received letters from members of the Lightning Brigade updating him on the brigade's actions. The 17th Indiana participated in skirmishes and small battles against Confederate forces in eastern Tennessee and north Alabama. In the meantime, General Bragg attempted to regain control of his army by suspending several officers who had been disrespectful, if not downright insubordinate, particularly in their disregarding his orders.

The Lightning Brigade was originally assigned to go to the Chattanooga area during the battle of Missionary Ridge in

---

[5] For a much more detailed account of the battle of Chickamauga, and Wilder's involvement in it, see Baumgartner's *Blue Lightning*.

[6] McGee, *History of the 72nd Indiana*, 195.

[7] Military letter, Samuel Munford, 22 September 1863, Greensburg-Decatur County Public Library (photocopy).

November 1863 but instead took part in destroying some Confederate wagons and stores in north Georgia. The brigade was eager to have Wilder back. Wilder undoubtedly spent autumn 1863 in Greensburg convalescing and attending to his business and whatever military affairs he could do from Indiana. By mid-December, his health restored, he was again fit enough to report back to his command, so he traveled south to rejoin his brigade. On Christmas 1863, Wilder was close to Huntsville, Alabama, with the 92nd Illinois, which called on Wilder to favor them with a speech. Although reluctant to do so, he did manage to convey that he appreciated the respect shown to him by the men. Friends back home in Indiana had sent food with Wilder for the Lightning Brigade, but Wilder treated the 92nd Illinois with this gift instead of his brigade.[8]

Wilder met up with the 72nd Indiana on 2 January 1864. The 72nd Indiana, extremely proud of Wilder, called their regimental battle flag "the Wilder flag."[9] Still concerned with military business and willing to return to battle, Wilder wrote to Nashville for supplies. He believed Forrest was planning to attack his troops and wanted to "entertain him," as he put it. However, he stated that his health was "but little improved."[10]

Many of the soldiers of the 17th Indiana re-enlisted in early January 1864, and the 17th was declared a veteran organization. In late January they were given leave to go back to their home state of Indiana where they were the honored guests at a reception at the capitol. Governor Oliver Morton and Wilder were both speakers at this event.

---

[8] Swedberg, ed., *Three Years with the 92nd Illinois*, 156–57.

[9] McGee, *History of the 72nd Indiana*, 244, 266.

[10] John T. Wilder letter, 27 January 1864, Greensburg-Decatur County Public Library (photocopy).

In April 1864, after convalescing in Indiana, Wilder was well enough to once again assume command of the Lightning Brigade, which had returned to Tennessee after their furlough. During May 1864, the Lightning Brigade marched south from Columbia, Tennessee, to Villanow, Georgia, choosing a route that took them through Trenton and Lafayette, Georgia. Wilder was once again looking for a fight but found none. In a letter to his wife, he reports his health now better than it had been in two years.[11] The improvement was short-lived, however, as Wilder soon found his health failing again. During this episode, in late May, Colonel A. O. Miller again took over command. Because of his dysentery, Wilder was forced to quit field service in mid-June 1864. From then until the end of the war, under the command of Colonel Jacob G. Vail, the 17th Indiana saw action in north Georgia and Alabama and at times pursued General John Bell Hood's troops north.

In early August 1864, Colonel John T. Wilder received the brevet rank of brigadier general. Even though Indiana governor Oliver Morton had presented Wilder's name to President Lincoln a year and a half earlier for a commissioned rank, the brevet rank is what he received, a lesser promotion than he had hoped for.[12] Brevet ranks were often given for gallantry and meritorious service, which Wilder had certainly given, but not necessarily for successful leadership, which Wilder also excelled in. They were also considered to be an honorary, instead of authoritative, promotion of rank and normally did not carry a raise of pay a regular promotion carried. At the end of the Civil War, the United States government issued many brevet ranks to officers, particularly senior offices, to recognize and reward

[11] John Wilder to Martha Wilder, 12 May 1864, John T. Wilder Papers, UTC.

[12] Baumgartner, *Blue Lightning*, 318.

their service. General Rosecrans had even sent Governor Morton a letter on 15 August 1863, recommending the promotion, in which he cited Wilder's "energy, ability, zeal, and sobriety."[13] Wilder had obviously earned a promotion, especially for his actions at Chickamauga.

Wilder was able to enjoy his promotion only a few months when his nagging health problems forced him to retire from service early in October 1864. His resignation order, Special Order 275, was dated 5 October, citing disability and being physically unsuitable.[14] His home life was certainly better. On New Year's Day 1865, his wife, Martha, gave birth to their third child, another girl, whom they named Rachel.

On 2 February 1865, Wilder was appointed by Governor Morton to the post of chief recruiting agent for the State of Indiana.[15] The war would be over in a matter of months, but the United States was not done with John T. Wilder. It appeared he still had plenty to offer his country, and he would serve his country again later in life.

In the four years that Wilder was in the Union Army, he acquitted himself admirably and showed success in leadership, resourcefulness, and ingenuity. He had been promoted several times. Having cut his teeth on military life and affairs in western Virginia, he received his first real test at Munfordville, Kentucky. There, his unorthodox but resourceful approach after being outnumbered, surrounded, and abandoned by his superiors prevented an enormous loss of life. He had the courage

---

[13] William S. Rosecrans to Oliver Morton, 15 August 1863 (photocopy), Greensburg-Decatur County Public Library.

[14] Military Document, Special Order 275, 5 October 1864 (photocopy), Greensburg-Decatur County Public Library.

[15] Indiana Adjutant General's Office Correspondence, W. H. H. Terrell, 2 February 1865, John T. Wilder Papers, UTC.

and determination not to surrender at the first inclination and opportunity. Wilder was also among the first officers from either side to exploit the effectiveness of the Spencer repeating rifles. He was also early to realize the efficacy of a mounted infantry, procuring horses, mostly without assistance from the government, for his troops. Wilder's men would do anything he asked of them, as shown by their aggressive and bold move at Hoover's Gap, Tennessee, during the Tullahoma Campaign. There, they helped push General Bragg and his Confederate troops further south, without the loss of a single soldier in his regiment. Finally, his actions during the bloody battle of Chickamauga showed that he was effective leader in the heat of battle, and, as a result, helped protect General George H. Thomas's troops in the Union defeat. Amazingly, Wilder accomplished all this while often sick. When looking back at the major Union leaders during the war, Wilder certainly does not compare with Generals Grant, Sherman, McClellan, Buell, and Halleck, to name a few of the more celebrated and better-known Union leaders (though some today are regarded in a lesser light). But he did leave his mark, and his legacy is still remembered today—in Indiana and Tennessee, and by countless Civil War buffs and historians who have realized the significance of Wilder's contributions, resourcefulness, and accomplishments during the conflict.

Chapter 7

Postwar: East Tennessee, the Roane Iron Company, Politics, and Travel

After the war ended in spring 1865, Wilder was back permanently in Greensburg, Indiana, and again focusing on his foundry. Both Union and Confederate soldiers were being demobilized. Former Confederate soldiers were required to sign an oath not to take up arms against the United States while Union troops were sent to rendezvous points to await formal processing and discharge. Confederate president Jefferson Davis was indicted but not convicted of treason and spent the next two years in a Virginia prison while Vice President Alexander Stephens spent five months in prison in Boston. Robert E. Lee was not imprisoned nor were any other Confederate officers.

The United States was at peace for the first time in four years, and the South entered a period defined as Reconstruction, a plan to reunite former Confederate states with the Union and to assist former slaves in their move to freedom and full citizenship. In Greensburg, Wilder built a large brick house to replace the house that was damaged in the fire of 1863. At that time, he apparently intended to remain in Indiana. However, when in Tennessee two years earlier, he had not failed to realize the rich resources of that region. That area, he now knew, was a mostly untapped resource for mines and foundries. The state's potential for industry was not a secret, either, as Tennessee state geologist Gerard Troost (1776–1850) noted in a report in 1840 that East Tennessee's rivers were sufficient to produce water needed to power factories and mills. Troost, who was born in the Netherlands, had been a minerology professor at the University of Nashville and, from 1831 to 1850, was the state geologist of Tennessee. Wilder was familiar with this report.

In 1865, Tennessee was still primarily an agricultural state as it had been prior to the war. There were mills already established, even some iron mills, but these were small compared to what Wilder began to envision. In the years immediately following the war, the Nashville press began to express the need for in-state factories and manufacturing, stating that a lack of factories would continue the state's dependence on Northern industries. Postwar reconstruction in Tennessee could not be carried out and supported just through its agricultural legacy. For example, cotton and wheat prices would decline through the late 1860s and into the 1870s.[1]

By the 1870s, attention would be directed to the vast resources of timber, coal, and iron ore present in the mountains of eastern Tennessee and Kentucky and western North Carolina. These resources became an important factor in rebuilding a new class structure in the South during the last decades of the nineteenth century.[2]

Soon after the war, several Appalachian states, including Kentucky, West Virginia, and Tennessee, began recruiting Northern investors, capitalists, and millwrights to develop industry in their states. To help attract them, they were offered attractive land ownership deals as well as other privileges. In the South, markets were unstable, interest rates were high, and few financial resources were available. Farmers who had suffered through the decline of crop prices now looked to industry as a way to make a living. Wilder's personal observations during the war made him aware of the industrial potential in

[1] Belissary, "Rise of Industry," 194–97.

[2] Eller, *Miners, Millhands, and Mountaineers*, 41.

Tennessee and the South. He likely also realized the lack of competition in the South from the dearth of mills and factories. Chattanooga appealed to Wilder, especially as it had never been entirely proslavery, and its citizens did not much resist nor resent the Union occupation.

Chattanooga first saw White settlement in the early 1800s, mostly from missionaries working with the native Cherokee Indians who, at that time, were situated in the southeastern United States. Several legends exist on the origin of the name *Chattanooga*. One popular explanation had *Chattanooga* being the Cherokee word for "large rock coming to a point." This was in reference to the northern end of Lookout Mountain that has its northernmost point of its eighty-mile length at the southern end of what is now Chattanooga. The earliest White settlement was a trading post on the Tennessee River called Ross's Landing, for John Ross, a wealthy local who was part Cherokee (one-eighth) and the principal-chief of the Cherokee Nation from 1828 to 1866. The city became known as Chattanooga in the late 1830s after the United States government forced many of the Cherokees in southeast Tennessee, north Georgia, and parts of North Carolina to what is now Oklahoma, a forced migration known today as the "Trail of Tears" for the disease, exhaustion, and high number of deaths among the Cherokee people as they traveled, mostly by foot, the hundreds of miles west. John Ross, as the principal-chief of the Cherokee Nation, had tried to stop this decree by the government but ultimately failed, and he, too, was forced to relocate to Indian Territory, which would become the state of Oklahoma in the early 1900s. His wife, Quatie, was one of those who died along the way. Ross's Landing served as one of several gathering posts the government created for the Cherokees prior to their orders to head west. After their removal, the city of

Chattanooga was incorporated in 1839. The town lies on the Tennessee River, on the Tennessee/Georgia border, approximately 120 miles north of Atlanta and 120 miles south of Nashville. It sits at a divide between the Appalachian Mountains and the Cumberland Plateau.

The city thrived from the start, mainly from the commerce it received via the Tennessee River, but when the Western and Atlantic Railroad arrived in 1850, the town began to grow, eventually reaching a population of several thousand inhabitants. Confederate forces held the city for the first two years of the Civil War, but in 1863 Rosecrans's Union forces with Wilder arrived and occupied the city and remained there until the end of the war.

Immediately following the war, the Union troops and officers left Chattanooga, leaving behind much of their property, equipment, and the facilities, buildings, and structures they built, including a fairly new rolling mill on the Tennessee River. The remnants of war were visible in Chattanooga when the war ended, with forts, earthworks, and a lack of greenery, due to trees having been felled in battle or for lumber. The battle of Missionary Ridge, just outside of Chattanooga at the time, left its mark. The victors claimed spoils as some homes of pro-Confederate citizens were seized by those brazen enough to do so, on the basis of delinquent taxes not been paid during the war. The delinquent tax forfeiture also provided cheap land, which enticed some Union soldiers and officers to remain or return to Chattanooga. Many of these Northerners had, however, a genuine desire to help Chattanooga recover and grow.

Wilder responded to the city's recruitment for Northern industrialists and decided in late 1865 or early 1866 to move his family and business to Chattanooga. An added bonus, along with the vast resources, was the warmer climate of Tennessee (as compared to Indiana). With his health still somewhat fragile, this milder climate also appealed to him. Only a few years after he had been part of an occupying force in the city, John T. Wilder became a citizen of it.

In 1866 Wilder and his family moved to Chattanooga, a town beginning its reconstruction process and to which many Northerners, especially those who served in the area during the war, were relocating. Chattanooga even solicited them, running an ad in a local paper that read, "Wanted Immediately Any Number of Carpet-Baggers to Come to Chattanooga to Settle." Another ad included the statement, "Those having capital, brains and muscle preferred."[3] Wilder built a large house on the side of Cameron Hill, a house that would rival the one he had built a year earlier back in Greensburg, Indiana, to replace the house damaged by fire while he was in the army. This was the same hill on which Eli Lilly, several years earlier, had set up his cannons to bomb downtown Chattanooga.

A good number of Northern industrialists and bankers did come to Chattanooga in the years following the war, and they are often referred to today (as they were back then) as carpetbaggers. But these workers were mostly welcomed in Chattanooga. However, it is debatable that they were all the carpetbagger prototype because many were not there to exploit the situation or to swindle the Southern locals; they were there by invitation to assist in the building up of Chattanooga and its industry, to make the city become what would later be called "the Dynamo of Dixie." Many who came focused not only on establishing business and industry but also on setting up a powerful base for city governance. By the early 1870s, the native Southerners of Chattanooga would see their power and control

[3] Govon and Livingood, *Chattanooga Country*, 287.

decrease in favor of the transplanted Northerners. Prior to the war, the city had been split between Democrats and Whigs. After the war, Tennessee became more Republican, led by "Parson" William G. Brownlow, who, first as governor (1865–1869) and then US senator (1869–1875), looked unfavorably toward the people and towns that had supported Tennessee secession. A former Methodist circuit rider, Brownlow was relentless in his attacks on his religious and political rivals, opponents, and critics, whom he attacked in the newspapers he published. Brownlow disenfranchised most supporters of the Confederacy in Chattanooga and throughout Tennessee by amending the city charter so as to make them ineligible to hold a public office or even to vote.

Chattanooga was invaded again by Northerners, this time in a more peaceful manner. Many came from the Midwest—Ohio, Illinois, and Indiana. These businessmen and industrialists who moved to Chattanooga and who fell into Wilder's circle formed an association that would last throughout the rest of the nineteenth century. They would play a major role in developing Chattanooga and bringing industry to southeast Tennessee and the southeastern United States.

Once Wilder was settled in Tennessee, he moved forward in resuming his industrial career. His success in Greensburg, Indiana, prior to the war proved to him that he would be successful in Tennessee as well. With Gerard Troost's geological reports to the Tennessee General Assembly, Wilder looked to the potential of the mountainous land that extended from Chattanooga more than a hundred miles north, known as the Cumberland Plateau. This was a region rich in iron ore and coal deposits, ideal for what Wilder needed for a foundry.[4]

[4] Moore, *Company Town*, 14.

Wilder set his sights on the resources in Roane County, seventy miles north of Chattanooga. Tennessee had become a state in 1796, and Roane County was formed five years later from a section of what was then Knox County and named after Archibald Roane, the second governor of Tennessee. The town of Kingston became the county seat. Leading up to the Civil War, Roane County was primarily agricultural, and, like Chattanooga, mostly pro-Union during the war. After the war, it also became a haven for Midwesterners to settle and help build up during Reconstruction.

An acquaintance of Wilder's from the war, Colonel Robert K. Byrd, a Southern Unionist from Tennessee, owned a farm in Roane County near the present town of Harriman. With his help, Wilder explored the area in spring 1866, riding his horse up and down the Cumberland Plateau and going as far south as the Georgia border. In the Unaka Mountains of East Tennessee, he found veins of brown hematite, and on Walden's Ridge he found coal in abundance. This, he realized, could be his answer to transportation costs, as these would also supply the minerals for railways.[5]

To help established an enterprise, Wilder turned to Hiram Sanborn Chamberlain, another Northerner who was also living in Chattanooga. Chamberlain, born in 1835 in Franklin, Ohio, was living in Knoxville at the war's conclusion. Chamberlain had grown up in Ohio and attended the Western Reserve Eclectic Institute in Hiram, which later became Hiram College. While attending the school, he was a friend to another student there, future president James A. Garfield. Chamberlain enlisted in the Union Army when the Civil War began and quickly earned the position of quarter-sergeant, and eventually second lieutenant and regimental quartermaster. As a member

[5] Ibid., 15.

of the 2nd Ohio Volunteer Cavalry, he was stationed at first in the west, in Kansas and Missouri. Eventually he ended up in Knoxville, Tennessee, as divisional quartermaster under General Ambrose Burnside. In 1864, he was promoted to captain and assistant quartermaster and served in that capacity until the war ended.[6]

Soon after the war ended, Chamberlain, along with a Welshman named Davey Richards, leased a rundown rolling mill in Knoxville, first naming it the Chamberlain and Richards. By 1867, it had grown, and, with the addition of more land, they incorporated it as the Knoxville Iron Company. Chamberlain, who had become acquainted with Wilder during the war, married into a prominent Knoxville industrial family, and this association would later open doors for Chamberlain and Wilder in mining circles in Tennessee.

In November 1865, even before Wilder had moved to Tennessee, he and Chamberlain traveled on horseback from Knoxville to an area that is now the town of Rockwood in Roane County. There they purchased 150 acres of land. This led to their establishing the East Tennessee Union Petroleum, Coal, Iron, and Salt Company.

A month after this acquisition Wilder, Chamberlain, and other associates, mostly other Northerners from Indiana and Ohio, founded the Roane Iron Company, with capital stock of $100,000. At first, the Roane Iron Company was a branch of the East Tennessee Union Petroleum, Coal, Iron, and Salt Company. Joining Wilder and Chamberlain in this venture were Henry C. Lord, David Rees, Antrim R. Forsyth, John M. Lord, and W.O. Rockwood.[7] These men were acquainted with

---

[6] Parkinson, "Hiram Sanborn Chamberlain," *Tennessee Encyclopedia*, https://tennesseeencyclopedia.net/entries/hiram-sanborn-chamberlain/.

[7] Henry C. Lord and John M. Lord apparently were not related.

Wilder prior to the war, either in business or militarily. They all hailed from the Midwest, most within one hundred miles of Wilder's foundry in Greensburg, Indiana. Forsyth was a businessman from Greensburg. Rockwood, whose son served under Wilder as an orderly during the war, was the largest stockholder in the company. Forsyth and Henry Lord had previously been involved with railroads in Indiana and Ohio and, like Wilder, envisioned railway possibilities in east Tennessee.[8] Rees was also from Indiana and appears to have looked after Wilder's business interests in Greensburg during the war.

According to the minutes of early corporate meetings, the Roane Iron Company was to be a legitimate business based on sound principles to allow the founders to invest in anticipation of realizing a reasonable profit.[9] Considering that they were already successful businessmen, particularly with railroads, they had reason to expect success in their new venture. In addition, local residents were more than willing to accept these Northerners into their region to develop industry. According to one local account, on the first day of construction, Wilder found several local men at the site with what appeared to be weapons. Fearing that Civil War hostilities still simmered in the region, he was greatly relieved to find that the men actually had brought tools and were observing the Southern custom of "lending a hand." To recruit and accommodate the workers, houses were quickly built, as well as a boarding house.

On 18 June 1867, W. O. Rockwood was elected the first president of the Roane Iron Company, at a salary of $1000 a year. Rockwood would remain president of the company until 1871. Wilder was made the general superintendent of the mill

---

[8] Moore, *Company Town*, 58.

[9] Roberts, "Roane Iron Company Establishes Rockwood after the Civil War," *Roane County News*, 3 February 1982.

and supervised the construction of the furnace. Among their earliest actions was the acquisition of land owned by Chamberlain and Rockwood, the issuance of $30,000 of capital stock to Wilder and Chamberlain, acquiring adjacent property, and the purchase of a sawmill from Wilder and Chamberlain.[10] Rockwood and John M. Lord built a "hot blast furnace," which was operational by 1 September 1868. For this they were to receive $40,000 in Roane Iron Company stock.

Between 1865 and 1869, Wilder and Chamberlain increased their property in Roane County by nearly two thousand acres of coal and iron-bearing land. They began with 928 acres, and in 1867 purchased one thousand additional acres. They would eventually come to own nearly twenty thousand acres in the area. With the addition of a portable sawmill, the first furnaces for the Roane Iron Company were constructed, as well as housing for the miners and crew. The small town, established in 1868, was named for W. O. Rockwood, despite that he never moved there or to Tennessee. Also in 1868 was the birth of the Wilders' fourth daughter. They named her Martha, after her mother.

The furnace at the Roane Iron Company became the first major blast furnace in the South. It was also the first in the South to use coke, the fuel derived from low-ash and low-bituminous coal, which at that time was considered to be a risky venture. By using scrap rails that were plentiful as well as inexpensive, the Roane Iron Company could produce iron rails cheap enough to rival those made by larger Northern mills.

The first furnace at the Roane Iron Company began producing pig iron in 1868 and by 1869 was producing fifteen tons a day, more than three times any other charcoal furnace

[10] Roberts, "Roane Iron is Important to Rockwood's History," *Roane County News*, 27 January 1982.

in the South.[11] To produce ore, they used red fossil hematite, available from nearby Walden's Ridge. Beehive coke ovens were placed near the furnace and fed from a nearby coal mine. Iron was hauled from the mine on a newly constructed narrow-gauge railway that led to the Tennessee River and then sent by barges and steamboats to Chattanooga and Knoxville, where it could be shipped to other markets. Due to its high phosphorous content, the pig iron produced foundry castings with a smooth surface, good for quality pipes, machine parts, and stove plates.

In a stockholder meeting on 26 October 1868, Wilder was directed, as superintendent, to arrange a contract for coal for the furnace and to settle with Lord and Rockwood for the construction of the completed furnace. Wilder also received added responsibilities, as amended in their bylaws, including a closer working relationship with the president of the company, W. O. Rockwood. Wilder was also given permission to purchase the right of way for a railway to the Tennessee River, as well as land for a warehouse and landing boats.

In 1869 Wilder acquired and added thirteen acres of land for the Roane Iron Company to be used as a river landing, as well as purchasing iron rights on adjacent land. His salary, as superintendent, was increased to $3000 annually. Wilder laid out and leased lots in Rockwood but prohibited the sale of dry goods, groceries, all articles of merchandise, and liquor, so as not to create competition with the company store.[12] In doing so, Wilder created the traditional "company town," a monopoly that many today look at as exploiting and controlling employees, who often were paid in company scrip—company

[11] Chamberlain, *Family Chronicle*, **[page?]**

[12] Roberts, "Roane Iron Company Establishes Rockwood after the Civil War," *Roane County News*, 3 February 1982.

issued currency—that usually was not exchangeable for goods, services, and wares outside of the company. It would be fair to compare Wilder to a robber baron, who gains wealth through exploiting workers and the resources they use or create. Despite this control, or perhaps because of it, it does not appear that Wilder ever saw any labor problems or strikes (or threats of) among his employees.

The Roane Iron Company worked to develop the town of Rockwood. When the mill opened, Rockwood had a population of three hundred. The 1870 census lists Rockwood with a population just under seven hundred, which includes 184 Black residents and 87 who were foreign-born. Tennessee-born residents numbered 363. The Roane Iron Company owned most of the houses in Rockwood, and a majority of them were in an area known as Miners Square. A church, school, and bank were also constructed. Wilder and his younger brother Horace both lived in Rockwood and played a big part in civic affairs of the city. Workers had a six-day work week, from ten to twelve hours a day, with Sundays off. The Black workers were used, if not preferred, for the heavier work.[13] The town grew slowly, and by 1880 the census listed just over one thousand citizens, with the foreign-born population down to nearly half of what it had been ten years earlier.

In 1870, the Roane Iron Company merged with the Southwestern Iron Company in Chattanooga, which had been established during the Civil War. Union general William T. Sherman had taken control of a mill that Confederate troops had originally built for the purpose of providing iron rails for railroads. After forcing the Confederate troops out of Chattanooga, Union forces completed construction of the mill to reroll iron rail and provide other metals for the Union Army. In

[13] Ezzell, *Chattanooga*, 18.

the years immediately following the Civil War, the rolling mill became the Southwestern Iron Company, run by a New Yorker, Abram S. Hewitt. This mill, on the Tennessee River in Chattanooga, had produced the first steel in the South.[14] By adding this new rolling mill, the Roane Iron Company became Chattanooga's biggest economic asset. After this merger, the Roane Iron Company was able to ship pig iron down the Tennessee River from Rockwood, and the mill in Chattanooga began producing iron rails of between fifty to sixty-five pounds weight per yard.

The Roane Iron Company increased its capital stock to $300,000 to take advantage of an offer to acquire four thousand acres of land. The company was then able to purchase the Vulcan Furnace Iron Lands from W. P. Rathburn and T. G. Montague, who later became directors in the Roane Iron Company.

In 1871, Rockwood resigned as president of the Roane Iron Company but was elected treasurer. W. P. Rathburn became the next president, and Hiram S. Chamberlain was elected vice president and general manager. In what would be repeated with many of Wilder's businesses, Wilder slowly phased out his involvement. He sold his property interests in the early 1870s and resigned as superintendent in 1875 to spend more time with other business and civic ventures. The company would use his knowledge and experience from time to time after that.[15] By the mid-1870s Roane County had grown but little. There were only two small towns, Kingston and Rockwood, each with a few churches and a substandard school.

---

[14] Chamberlain, *Family Chronicle*, 8.

[15] Moore, *Company Town*, 22.

In 1871, just five years after Wilder became a citizen of Chattanooga, he had risen to the point he was accepted and respected enough to be elected mayor of the city. During this period, mayors in Chattanooga served only one-year terms and held very little power. A board of aldermen made up of two citizens from each of the four wards of the town wielded most of the control in the city.

In the first years of Reconstruction, President Andrew Johnson, a Southerner from Tennessee who had stayed loyal to the Union during the war and served as President Lincoln's vice president in 1864 and 1865, attempted to enact Reconstruction laws that would allow Southern states to determine what rights the former slaves would have. Northern Republicans resisted such laws, feeling they gave Southern Whites, particularly former Confederate soldiers and officers, too much power in handling the freed slaves.

During Reconstruction in Chattanooga, the city saw a rise of Southern Democrats, known as "Bourbon Democrats," who were resistant to both the rising role of Black citizens in the city as well as to the increase of Northerners and Midwesterners in general, despite their having been recruited and welcomed to the city. Due to the patronage system, in which positions were awarded to political supporters and allies, a number of Black men were appointed to government positions while others were elected to city office. Such was the political scene of Chattanooga in the early 1870s when Wilder was mayor.

Wilder, running as a Republican for the office, defeated Thomas Webster, who, like Wilder, was a foundry owner. The *Knoxville Daily Chronicle* reported on his election,

> There is better material [now] in this Board than we have ever had since the war. They were elected when the people were aroused to the necessity for action, and we hope the

> same interest in progress and reform will be maintained throughout the year that has been manifested in this election. General Wilder is a pronounced Republican, and a thoroughly live man, and under his administration we hope Chattanooga will arrive at the summit [of] wealth and prosperity. The General was once taunted with being a carpetbagger, and admitted the fact, but added that his carpet-bag weighed several tons. But the citizens of Chattanooga know his worth and show their appreciation of it by electing him to manage their affairs, and in doing so they have made a most excellent choice.[16]

Despite the Bourbon Democrats' trying to quash the industrialization brought by Northern businesses, a pattern was emerging in the city: Northerners who moved to Chattanooga in the years immediately after the war, like Wilder and his business partners, did well when running for local offices.[17] As mayor, Wilder followed William P. Rathburn, originally from Ohio, who would later get involved with the Roane Iron Company. Wilder did not serve out his full one-year term, resigning in May 1872. In the six months he had been mayor, Wilder had attended only one meeting of aldermen. The position of mayor was interfering with his business interests, and he was also still involved with the Roane Iron Company. Upon Wilder's resignation, an alderman of the city, Josiah Jackson Bryan, was elected to replace him and served out his term.

Despite not completing his term as mayor, Wilder did manage to accomplish some things during his months in office. He established the free school system in Chattanooga. He was also instrumental in implementing the "four mile law" which made it illegal to have a saloon or enterprise that sold whiskey

---

[16] *Knoxville Daily Chronicle*, 18 November 1871.

[17] Govan and Livingood, *Chattanooga Country*, 286.

within four miles of a school or an iron mill. Wilder, a staunch teetotaler, was dedicated to making sure the city's workers did not become drunkards.

Perhaps Wilder was finished with politics for the time being, despite southeastern Tennessee citizens encouraging him to run for Congress in 1872. A notice in the *Chattanooga Herald* reported the fact, stating the endorsement of many locals and their request:

> Believing that the material interests of this portion of the State demand the selection of a most able and efficient Representative in Congress from this District, and believing you to be preeminently qualified for that important position, the undersigned respectfully request you to permit the announcement of your name as a candidate for the Third District, at the next general election.[18]

Despite their wishes, Wilder did not throw his hat in the ring.

It was also during this time, later in 1872, that Wilder and his wife finally saw the arrival of a son after four daughters. Stuart (possibly named after Martha's maiden name of Stewart) would be the couple's only son. Their sixth and last child, a fifth daughter named Edith, would be born in late 1875.

With the success of the Roane Iron Company, Wilder looked to Europe for the possibility of expanding his mills, to acquire minerals, and for importing products. A full-fledged industrialist, Wilder also explored ways to promote his interests and businesses. He traveled to England and Europe in 1873 and again in 1874 to check out the possibilities. Wilder acted as the Tennessee commissioner to the 1873 World's Fair held in Vienna, Austria. Austria was eager to show the world its reconstruction and progress after its 1866 war with Prussia, and

[18] *Knoxville Daily Chronicle*, 25 April 1872.

1873 would also coincide with the twenty-fifth anniversary of the coronation of Emperor Franz Joseph. One of the major themes of the exposition was the industrial age, especially in mining and engineering, which was well-suited for Wilder. He reported that he had secured a prime location of "one hundred feet square at the entrance of the American wing" at the World's Fair.[19] In the 1879 publication "Report of Committee to Investigate the Agricultural Bureau, to the Forty-First General Assembly of the State of Tennessee," Wilder states that in 1873 he took ten tons of ore to Vienna and with it displayed the largest lump of coal ever seen. He also took several thousand copies of books and reports by Joseph B. Killebrew, Tennessee's commissioner of agriculture, on Tennessee's agricultural and industrial resources, thus introducing to Europe all that Tennessee had to offer. In this same report, Wilder claimed, perhaps even exaggerated, to have visited seven hundred English iron works the following year.[20] Aside from Wilder's involvement, the United States was not well represented at the fair, and the American representatives that attended seemed more interested in gleaning ideas for the next world's fair in Philadelphia, to be held in 1876.

Wilder's introduction of Tennessee resources in Vienna in 1873 seems to have paid off. In May 1874, Wilder received a letter from American manufacturer and importer George W. Silcox, inquiring as to the possibility of Wilder providing iron for the purpose of making ships for buyers Silcox had located in Odessa, Constantinople, and Copenhagen.[21] Wilder's 1874 visit to England is also proven by the fact that in the John T.

---

[19] *Memphis Public Ledger*, 12 April 1873.

[20] *House Journal of the First Session*, 560–61.

[21] George W. Silcox to John Wilder, 26 May 1874, John T. Wilder Papers, UTC.

Wilder collection at the University of Tennessee at Chattanooga, there is a card admitting "bearer" to the House of Lords for July 1874. Wilder apparently became acquainted with noble-born English citizens because this collection also contains correspondence to Wilder in which someone with a title is mentioned in somewhat familiar terms, and as recommending governesses for his children. Online resources show the passenger manifest for the ship *Oceanic* in early 1874, and that a John Wilder, aged forty-four, was a passenger. This was a New York to Liverpool, England, route. This coincides both with Wilder's age and his time in England.

As Wilder developed his mining interests, other American cities saw a boom in industrialization. The natural resources were abundant, and investors and industrialists in both America and Europe saw the potential in the American South. Birmingham, Alabama, like Chattanooga, grew as industry developed, and other Northerners came south to take advantage of the possibilities as Wilder had done in 1866. In 1876, Wilder, along with Hiram S. Chamberlain and H. Clay Evans, formed another company, the Coal, Iron, and Manufacturers Association, with the intent to further develop industry in the region. They also hosted other industrial and engineering association meetings.[22]

Again involved with a World's Fair, this time in Philadelphia in 1876, Wilder was one of only six Tennesseans appointed by the governor to manage state exhibits, and he sent Tennessee minerals to be displayed. The 1876 World's Fair (also known as the Centennial Exhibition in commemoration of the hundredth anniversary of the signing of the Declaration of Independence in Philadelphia) is noted for several important events. It was during this exposition that Alexander Graham

[22] Ezzell, *Chattanooga*, 59.

Bell first exhibited the telephone; the typewriter was first introduced; Thomas Edison presented his first phonograph; and a condiment called ketchup made its first appearance. Samuel Cole Williams, in his biography of Wilder, claims a friendship existed between Wilder and Alexander Graham Bell, but Wilder declined to invest in Bell's telephone. If this is true, it is possible they became acquainted at the 1876 World's Fair since there seem to be no other events in Wilder's life where they might have crossed paths.[23]

In addition to having served Chattanooga as mayor, Wilder also served as postmaster to the city starting in late October 1877. Unlike the role of mayor, this position carried more weight and responsibility as the postmaster ran the post office and ensured mail services were running efficiently. It was also a political appointment, made by the first assistant postmaster general and endorsed by the president, who was, during this period, Rutherford B. Hayes. The normal duties included inventorying the office, keeping the office open during the normal hours (and even working on Sunday to attend to the arrival of mail that day), sorting and bundling the mail daily, and completing all paperwork and reports. The postmaster could also appoint an assistant postmaster to attend to the duties when he was unable to.[24] With myriad businesses and projects in which Wilder was involved, it seems unlikely he would have had the time to fully attend the duties and meet expectations of the typical postmaster of the era. Wilder, though, served as Chattanooga's postmaster until 1882. Who assisted him as he went about his businesses is not documented, but during the years Wilder served as postmaster of Chattanooga he

[23] Biographies on Bell that were consulted do not mention any relationship or association with Wilder.

[24] Prechtel-Kluskens, "Nineteenth-Century Postmaster," 33–35.

undoubtedly had someone assist him, if not handle the lion's share of the duties, as he became involved with other projects, especially some that took him to northeastern Tennessee.

Living in Chattanooga, Wilder stepped back into his Civil War persona long enough to help his adopted hometown. A Confederate memorial in Chattanooga had suffered vandalism. The local Confederate veterans were shocked at the damage done to the memorial and plans were made to erect a wall around the memorial to prevent further vandalism. Wilder enlisted the help of other local Union veterans to assist with the project, paid for restoration of the damaged memorial, and arranged for a protective wall to be constructed. If Wilder had not yet won the respect and friendship of Confederate veterans in the area, this was probably the beginning of a relationship that lasted the rest of Wilder's life.[25]

In the years following the war, Wilder found ways to continue serving his government. A story that appears in several sources, including Williams's biography of Wilder, describes how Wilder, at the behest of the United States government and President Ulysses Grant, personally ascertained from his old nemesis Nathan Bedford Forrest his involvement with the recently formed Ku Klux Klan. (Williams dates the account to 1865, but other accounts estimate it was the early 1870s, which is more likely, as this was at the time Ulysses Grant was president.) This account also appeared in a 1901 article in the *Memphis Daily Appeal*, which stated, "[Forrest] sent to President Grant though former Governor and now Senator Oliver P.

[25] Ezzell, *Chattanooga*, 24.

Morton of Indiana and Gen. John T. Wilder full information as to his connection with the affair…."[26]

Wilder heard that the government was investigating Forrest, the former Confederate general, for violating the conditions of the parole given ex-Confederate soldiers and officers, by associating with (or even playing a bigger role such as founding) the pro-Southern vigilante group, which sprung up in Tennessee in the years following the war. Forrest had been a dashing, cagey, and violent Confederate cavalry leader during the war despite having no formal military training, like Wilder. Forrest had enlisted early in the war as a private; by war's end he was a lieutenant general. Forrest's reputation began to suffer after the battle at Fort Pillow in Tennessee in April 1864. There, men under Forrest's command, in what can only be described as a massacre, killed approximately 250 Black Union soldiers without making any attempt at capturing them. The accusations were that Forrest gave explicit orders to shoot any and all Black Union soldiers. Nearly three hundred White Union soldiers, many Tennesseans, also were killed. In the first years after the war, Forrest had been involved in the founding of the Ku Klux Klan, and some believe he was even the first Grand Wizard.

Wilder traveled to Memphis to meet with Forrest to determine his involvement with the Klan. Forrest apparently convinced Wilder his objectives with the organization were not as others had thought or feared and told Wilder he was only acting in the best interest and protection of the Southern people. For whatever reason, Wilder took Forrest at his word and subsequently traveled to Washington to convince President Grant

[26] Ashdown and Caudill, *Myth of Nathan Bedford Forrest*, 92. Biographies of Forrest consulted did not mention nor confirm a post-war friendship between Forrest and Wilder.

that General Forrest had not violated any conditions for parole. Former Indiana governor Oliver Morton, as well as General John A. Logan, also vouched for General Forrest. President Grant evidently was satisfied with Wilder's explanation, and no warrant was issued for General Forrest's arrest. Perhaps a friendship was created, as Wilder was to say later that Forrest even once paid him a visit in Chattanooga and stayed a week at his home.[27]

[27] Williams, *Wilder*, 50.

Chapter 8

The Cloudland Hotel, Railroads, and Other Affairs

Roan Mountain in northeastern Tennessee rises to a height of 6285 feet, and the state line separating Tennessee and North Carolina runs right over its summit. It is part of a range of hundreds of mountain peaks of the Appalachian Mountains and north of the range known as the Smoky Mountains.[1] One of its many appeals is the wild rhododendrons that bloom over the mountains in the early summer. Purple Catawba, pink Maxim, and white Carolina rhododendrons bloom every June, covering the normally dark green mountaintops in color. The top of Roan Mountain is also covered by many balsam fir trees, rare this far south in the United States but able to grow due to the high altitude of the mountaintops, also rare for this region.

In the late 1870s, Wilder, in search of better veins of iron ore, had developed a small mine in nearby North Carolina, just across the Tennessee border into Mitchell County, at a location he called the Magnetic City and that eventually became known as Buladean. Despite being Chattanooga's postmaster, Wilder was also venturing out, taking over and developing a network of small mines in northeast Tennessee and western North Carolina, a mountainous region north of today's Smoky Mountain National Park. This region in North Carolina, Wilder discovered, yielded large deposits of magnetite. Because the ore in the area around the Roane Iron Company contained too much

---

[1] Despite similarity in names, Roan Mountain is not in Roane County, Tennessee, and is approximately 175 miles east of Rockwood where the Roane Iron Company was located.

sulfur, it could not produce the strong iron he needed for railroad wheels and rails. This region near Buladean would provide the necessary minerals he needed to do that. Wilder, along with several business partners, had purchased several hundred thousand acres of land in North Carolina, Tennessee, Kentucky, and Virginia.[2] Wilder had also bought into a mine in nearby Cranberry, North Carolina, called the Cranberry Mine, which was producing magnetic iron. The ore there contained no sulfur, thus making it more suitable for railway iron. To help with the transporting of the ore, Wilder put in a railway line to haul the ore from the mines to nearby Johnson City, Tennessee. Wilder also developed a small mine, known then as the "Peg Leg Mine" in what is now Roan Mountain State Park. Not stopping there, Wilder also opened another small mine between Elk Ridge and Shell Creek Station, Tennessee, in 1880. These were just some of the many small mines Wilder developed across the region.

In the 1870s, Wilder purchased land for $8,000 and built the small Tennessee town of Roan Mountain, which he named after the nearby mountain, approximately thirty miles east of Johnson City, Tennessee. He laid out the streets and named them and even built the first church, despite not being particularly religious himself. Because he was always entertaining guests and family, Wilder built a small, three-story inn for accommodations, calling it the Roan Mountain Inn. Before long, Wilder realized that an inn higher up on Roan Mountain, even near the top, might attract more seasonal visitors because the absence of pollen at that altitude would be ideal for hay fever sufferers. The cooler temperatures would certainly be a draw, especially to Southerners, who wouldn't see air conditioning in

---

[2] McCoy, "Roan's Cloudland Hotel Famous in 19th Century," *Asheville Citizen*, 11 June 1950.

their homes and buildings for several more decades. The elevation was also too high for bothersome insects and poisonous snakes. In 1877, Wilder and an associate named L. B. Searle, a contractor also from Chattanooga, built their first inn near the top of Roan Mountain, with several dozen rooms to accommodate guests. Perhaps he wanted to bring a bit of his boyhood home of the Catskill Mountains and their spacious hotels to Tennessee. This location offered cool summer temperatures, averaging sixty degrees during daytime, and offered a great view, which was said to overlook seven states. Visitors to the mountain soon became known as the Hay Fever Brigade. The location also afforded two unusual phenomena—a strange humming sound that got labeled as "mountain music," and circular rainbows when there were storms.

In 1885, Wilder opened a second, larger hotel on Roan Mountain near the first inn. To avoid having to haul construction lumber up several thousand feet, he used the balsam trees on the mountain for the necessary lumber.[3] Because of the frequent clouds near the top of Roan Mountain (and the belief that this was one of the only places on earth you could see your shadow in the clouds), the locals had named the top of the mountain "Cloudland." Wilder named this new hotel the Cloudland Hotel, and it sat near the mountaintop. This was a three-story hotel with several hundred rooms.[4] Some reports stated it could accommodate up to a thousand guests. It was not a "grand hotel" in any sense—it appears quite plain, though large, in extant exterior photographs. No pictures of

---

[3] Jeeter Goudge interview, Ron D. Vance and Barbara H. Wickerson Collection, Acc. 621, Archives of Appalachia, East Tennessee State University.

[4] The reported number of rooms varies from different accounts, but some have it as large as 365 rooms.

the inside are known to exist, so it is not known if it was fancy or had elegant furniture. Of note is the fact that there was only one privy in the hotel although the rooms had their own copper bathtubs. The Cloudland Hotel was L-shaped, and each wing was two hundred feet long and forty-two feet wide, and the state line dividing Tennessee and North Carolina passed through the middle of the hotel. Liquor was legal in Tennessee but illegal in North Carolina, so guests had to be careful where they imbibed, or even walked inside the hotel, drink in hand. Local lore states that occasionally a sheriff stood guard, hoping to catch careless drinkers as they accidentally crossed a room into the North Carolina side. A state line was drawn down the middle of the dining room and even divided the large dining table. It was even said that some guests slept with their heads in Tennessee and their feet in North Carolina.

To get to the Cloudland Hotel, a road was built from the town of Roan Mountain up the mountain to the hotel. A local worker, Rube Mosely, oversaw a group of workers who built the road and cut down the trees used for lumber on the hotel.[5] There were two carriage trips up the mountain a day. Guests arrived at the town of Roan Mountain on "The Tweetsie"—the East Tennessee and Western North Carolina Railroad, a narrow gauge "stemwinder" that ran from Johnson City, Tennessee, to the Cranberry mines in western North Carolina. They might first stay at the Roan Mountain Inn and then could take one of the carriages up to the Cloudland Hotel, a trip that would take several hours. The cost for staying at the Cloudland Hotel was $2 a day, $10 a week, or $30 a month.[6] Because of the difficulty getting to the inn and the remoteness

---

[5] Sheppard, *Cabins in the Laurel*, 85.

[6] "Cloudland Hotel...Only Memories Remain," *Elizabethton (TN) Star*, 18 June 1995.

of the area, most guests stayed at least two weeks, with many staying the entire season, which ran from late June to September. To enhance his guests' visits, Wilder put in a croquet lawn, tennis courts, golf course, several ponds, and a dance floor in the hotel basement. Because of the high altitude, custom golf balls were furnished to accommodate the thinner air. In addition to the single (but hopefully large) restroom inside the hotel, there were also several outhouses. A laundry was available for the guests, and water was pumped up from a nearby spring, with a furnace providing heated water for the hotel. Guests in the dining room were waited on by attractive young girls imported from Asheville, North Carolina, and there were two cooks, a pastry cook, several chambermaids, and two bellboys. Cattle were brought up and herded nearby and slaughtered as needed for food.

A flyer from that period invited guests to "come up out of the sultry plains to the 'land of the sky'—magnificent views above the clouds where rivers are born—a most extended prospect of 50,000 square miles in seven different states—one hundred mountain tops over 4,000 feet high, in sight." The flyer also boasted "clear cold water, only thirteen degrees above freezing; beautiful brooks teeming with mountain trout, summer temperatures from forty-eight to seventy-three degrees (usually sixty degrees); the most even temperature known—balmy, bracing air, its like can not be found by going North; a clean, healthful, pleasant, beautiful summer resort. Try it."

According to local lore, botanists Asa Gray and Andre Michaux, poet James Whitcomb Riley, and merchant and US postmaster John Wannamaker are all believed to have been guests.[7] Other accounts state that royalty (unnamed) from Europe also stayed at the hotel.[8]

An amusing anecdote, related by Wilder's great-grandson, Thomas Maher, and evidently passed down orally in the family, recounts Wilder's arrival at the hotel one evening, wet and muddy from a long horse ride. In the dining room, the waitress, unaware of who he was, at first resisted serving him. She then relented and produced some corn for his horse, at Wilder's request. "Here's the corn for your horse," she told him. "I put some in for you 'cause you eat like one and you smell like one, too!" This amused Wilder so much that he gave the waitress a $5 tip.[9]

Wilder employed managers to run the Cloudland, and some did better than others. A few, unfortunately, drank the money away that Wilder sent for upkeep, which must have annoyed Wilder, a nondrinker, immensely. After several years, the hotel began to deteriorate, and Wilder sold out and left the area to pursue other interests. The hotel continued to operate into the twentieth century, but by 1920 it was closed for good. Everything that could be taken was sold and hauled away, including the wood of the hotel itself. In only a few decades, nothing remained of the Cloudland Hotel but the foundation. Many a house in eastern Tennessee and western North

---

[7] Margaret Probst and Florence Graybeal interview, Ron D. Vance and Barbara H. Wickerson Collection, Acc. 621, Archives of Appalachia, East Tennessee State University.

[8] Wilson, *Roan Mountain: A Passage of Time* (Winston-Salem, NC: John F.Blair, 1991) 96.

[9] Maher, "Roan Mountain and Gen. John T. Wilder," 6.

Carolina were either built from wood from the Cloudland or had furniture from the hotel interior.[10]

Even though Wilder had homes in various towns in Tennessee, his nice house on Cameron Hill in downtown Chattanooga was his home base. In 1880, Wilder, always looking for a new venture, started up a machine factory in Chattanooga, which he named Wilder's Machine Works. Among the items he produced was the turbine wheel he had invented before the Civil War.[11] Perhaps his duties as postmaster were too much for him; he leased the company away the following year, and the name was changed to the Lowe Machine Works.

Several years after the Civil War ended, Chattanooga businessmen, along with local Methodist ministers, began discussing the desire and need for a central university in the South. In 1872, an education conference was held in Knoxville, and a local educator, Professor Percival C. Wilson, presented a paper proposing a central university for the Methodist Episcopal Church in the South. The Methodist Church had sent representatives from its seven conferences in the central South, which included parts of Tennessee, Alabama, Georgia, Kentucky, and Virginia. Professor Wilson's paper was well received, and the following month in Cleveland, Tennessee, the proposal was presented at the Holston Conference, the local Methodist conference of the region. Even though the University of the South, an Episcopal school, was fifty miles northwest in Sewanee, and a Methodist university, East Tennessee Wesleyan University, was sixty miles to the northeast in Athens, Tennessee, the church organized committees of interested

---

[10] Today, remnants of the foundation can still be found at the site. There is a modern parking lot, a sign, and access to the Appalachian Trail, which is close to the site.

[11] Williams, *Wilder*, 43.

citizens and charged them to proceed in forming a university. It was quickly determined that the school needed to be in Chattanooga. As an influential citizen of Chattanooga, John T. Wilder was part of this group. With the help of the Methodist Church, their dreams were realized, although it would take fourteen years to open the school.

Chattanooga University opened in fall 1886, enrolling over one hundred students for its first term. Shortly before the school opened, the school building was completed, an impressive multistory building that was quickly named "Old Main." A board of directors was selected and included prominent Chattanooga citizens Hiram S. Chamberlain and David Rees, both businessmen associated with Wilder. Wilder was one of thirty-seven original trustees of the university and served in that capacity for two years. Chattanooga University struggled in its first two years, primarily over the issue of whether it would enroll Black students. Despite receiving support and funding from the Freedman's Aid Society, the local school administrators were adamant in not allowing Black students to attend. The then-Northern-based Methodist Church tried unsuccessfully to force the school to enroll Black students, so the fear among local students that they would soon be sitting alongside Black students persisted, and enrollment suffered.[12] To help the school survive, the Methodist Church decided in 1889 to merge Chattanooga University with Grant Memorial University (originally East Tennessee Wesleyan University, renamed by the Methodist Church upon Grant's death to honor him). The two schools were renamed U. S. Grant University, so it wouldn't look as if they (Chattanooga) had been consumed by an existing school. The school now had two campuses—

[12] See Govan and Livingood, *University of Chattanooga*, 44. The school did not enroll Black students until the mid-1960s.

Chattanooga and Athens. Several decades later, the two schools eventually split, with the Athens branch becoming today's Tennessee Wesleyan College and the Chattanooga campus becoming the University of Chattanooga. The University of Chattanooga joined the University of Tennessee system in 1969 to become the University of Tennessee at Chattanooga, which it remains today. Even though Wilder was an original trustee, university records reveal no personal involvement of Wilder in the planning of the university or in its first years, and alumni registers do not show that any of his children attended. It is probable that Wilder, as he appears to have done with other ventures, merely lent his name and endorsement to the project. His business partner, Hiram S. Chamberlain, was more involved, and the original athletic field—Chamberlain Field—was named after him. The school's baseball and football teams played on the field, and the football team played on it until the 1990s. Recent renovations to the campus have since removed most signs that a football gridiron was once on the site, and the football team now plays at a city athletic field and stadium several miles off campus.

Wilder's political career did not end with his brief stint as mayor of Chattanooga in 1871. In 1886, while planning to enter the railroad business (and apparently involved with the university in Chattanooga), Wilder also ran for Congress, again as a Republican. Even though the race was close, he did not win.[13] Democrats had controlled the seat ever since another Chattanooga politician, William Crutchfield, held it from 1872 to 1873. Since 1874, Democrats had won the seat with large margins, which had started to decline with the 1882 election. Democrats had also held the Tennessee governor's seat since 1871, with the exception of 1881–1883. Wilder narrowly

[13] Williams's biography erroneously gives the year as 1876.

lost his race for Congress to the incumbent, John Randolph Neal, 14,115 votes to 13,768, a margin of 50.6 percent of the vote to Wilder's 49.4 percent.[14] There's no record of what Wilder's intent was for running for office, if he was cajoled into running, or how interested he was in the seat. Considering his incomplete term as mayor and his several ongoing business and mining ventures in 1886, one has to wonder how he would have found the time to serve as a congressman had he been elected.[15] In the next election, 1888, the Democrats did lose the seat, and a former Chattanooga mayor, H. Clay Evans, was elected in another closely contested election. During this period, Wilder was still involved in his foundries and mining interests, and he was still developing tools and equipment for his work. An 1879 patent reveals another turbine water wheel was registered by Wilder.[16]

It isn't documented if Wilder was actually in Chattanooga or on the Chattanooga University campus on its opening day in September 1886, but there was a good chance he wasn't since he was involved with another of his enterprises at the time. In the effort to provide a link between coal fields in Virginia and Kentucky and to move that product north and south, Wilder, in 1886, established a railroad that could provide these services. In late September 1886, Wilder began developing the Charleston, Cincinnati & Chicago Railroad Company, which would soon be known at the "3-Cs" or "Triple C." The original plan was for the line to extend for more than six hundred miles,

---

[14] *Congressional Quarterly's Guide to U.S. Elections*, 1081.

[15] From 1971 until 2007, the state of Tennessee had as its lieutenant governor a man named John Shelton Wilder. Genealogies on Ancestry.com indicate that John T. Wilder and John S. Wilder were very distantly related, both being descended from Edward Wilder (1623–1690) of Hingham, Massachusetts, mentioned earlier.

[16] American Institute of Mining Engineers, "New Patents," 242.

from Ironton, Ohio, to Charleston, South Carolina. With this route, it could cover the agriculture of the piedmont, timber, and coal regions of Virginia and Kentucky as well as the resort areas of eastern Tennessee and western North Carolina. Wilder, no doubt, realized it could also bring visitors to his Cloudland Hotel on Roan Mountain.[17] The railroad would have terminals on the Ohio River and the coast at Charleston. Along its route, it could meet up with other railways for transfer of materials. The cost of the 3-Cs was estimated to run over $21 million. Unfortunately, one of the main backers of this railroad was the British banking firm Baring Brothers, which would collapse during a depression in the early 1890s.

On 14 January 1887, Wilder held a meeting in Camden, South Carolina, for local citizens, the purpose being to raise funds for his railroad. Wilder described to the audience the route of the railway, from Charleston to Camden, up to Ashland, Kentucky.[18] He guaranteed that coal would be delivered to Charleston for $3 a ton, making that city the top coaling port in the South. Wilder knew the route well and realized that the area would provide iron ore needed to make Bessemer steel. He also intended to build blast furnaces and rolling mills at various points along the way. Groundbreaking was on 14 March 1887.[19] The 3-Cs rail line would add existing lines built by the Rutherford Railway Construction Company several years earlier. A rail line was built from Marion, North Carolina to Kingville, North Carolina, and from Johnson City, Tennessee, south to the small community of Chestoa, Tennessee,

---

[17] This also coincides with the time Wilder ran unsuccessfully for Congress. How he would have found the time to be a congressman is puzzling, given he was involved in several business ventures at the time.

[18] Goforth, *Building the Clinchfield*, 12.

[19] Way Jr., *Clinchfield Railroad*, 55–60.

approximately twenty-five miles south of Johnson City. Portions of the railroad were operable by late 1888. In 1889, Wilder purchased land in Blacksburg, South Carolina, no doubt in hopes of running his railway through there and benefiting from the rich Bessemer ore found in that area. This, he felt, would be an ideal spot for a new foundry.

Construction on the 3-Cs continued over several years but was halted from the great panic of 1893, when the Baring Brothers became insolvent. Wilder would suffer financially as a result.[20] The 3-Cs line was sold that year, and its remnants would be used to develop the Ohio River and Charleston Railroad.

[20] Ibid., 86. Years later, the company was revived without Wilder and reorganized as the South and Western Railroad.

Chapter 9

Memorializing: A Return to Service and Duty

Sixteen years after the end of the Civil War, and eighteen years after the battles of Chickamauga and Chattanooga, the Society of the Army of the Cumberland, made up of veterans of the Union Army of the Cumberland, held a reunion in Chattanooga. Reunions, begun in 1868 in Cincinnati, in the following years had been held in cities mostly in the Midwest such as Chicago, Cleveland, Indianapolis, and Toledo. In 1881, the organization held the reunion in Chattanooga, the first time the organization held a reunion in the South.

In September 1881, the veterans eagerly reunited in Chattanooga. Despite mourning the death of President James Garfield the day before, who had lingered after being shot by an assassin two and a half months earlier, veterans from both Union and Confederate sides mingled and visited, and John Wilder was part of this reunion. Included in the event was a short journey to the Chickamauga battlefield in north Georgia. Upon arrival, and after exploring the area, many veterans were surprised and shocked at how overgrown the battlefield had become in eighteen years, making it difficult to locate specific areas important in the battle. It was there that an idea began to germinate: the preservation of battlefields as national landmarks. Many veterans felt strongly about such designation and would continue this sentiment and discussion for several years.

In 1888, newspaperman Henry V. Boynton, a veteran of the Army of the Cumberland, wrote a series of articles suggesting that the sites should be preserved. Boynton had recently visited the Chickamauga battlefield, and his interest in preserving the site grew from this visit. Boynton had been awarded the Medal of Honor for his actions leading the Ohio 35th Infantry at the Battle of Missionary Ridge in November 1863. After the war, Boynton had become a newspaper correspondent in Washington, D.C. Both Union and Confederate veterans enthusiastically agreed with Boynton. Boynton pitched the idea at that year's reunion of the Army of the Cumberland, which was held in Chicago. As a result of Boynton's interest, the Chickamauga Memorial Association was formed, with Boynton appointed chairman. The next year, 1889, brought the Army of the Cumberland back to Chattanooga for another reunion. The main theme for this reunion was the preservation of the local battlefields, which included Missionary Ridge and Orchard Knob in Chattanooga, both important battle sites in fall 1863. On 20 September 1889, a meeting was held on the Chickamauga battlefield, and John Wilder was elected president of the newly formed memorial organization. Several months later, on 4 December, a charter for the Chickamauga Memorial Association was granted by the state of Georgia. The following year, on 18 August 1890, President Benjamin Harrison signed the act, which made the Chickamauga and Chattanooga National Military Park the first national military park in the United States.

After a quarter of a century, the rural countryside that had been battlefields of bloody, violent warfare was just beginning to be preserved and memorialized. By the 1890s, soldiers from both the North and the South would work together to document for posterity the sites where many of their friends, relatives, and comrades had fallen. Many of these soldiers, having fought in their late teens or early twenties, were not yet fifty years of age. Officers, many who had seen their first combat in the Mexican-American War of the late 1840s, were older, and had already begun dying off. Gettysburg, in Pennsylvania, had been among the first battlefields preserved. Soon, other major battlefields such as Shiloh, Vicksburg, and Antietam would see their veterans meet in peace to honor and respect the site and their fallen comrades and, perhaps for the first time, to honor even their fallen adversaries. They had the advantage, only several decades after the war, of the still undeveloped battlefields, where industry and growing city sprawl had yet to invade. Also helpful was the fact that Congress and state governments by the 1890s were populated with veterans of the war who were willing to allot funding for such a cause. This was, as historian Timothy B. Smith called it, the "Golden Age of Civil War Battlefield Preservation."[1] The Chickamauga and Chattanooga sites were included in these national preservation efforts. Surviving soldiers from the Union and Confederate Armies would work together to preserve the sites where they as young men gave their all, some the last full measure, and where they faced and witnessed death, and endured countless horrors, injuries, and heartbreak. These battlefields, in the 1890s, would offer a site to begin and perhaps complete the reconciliation.

Battlefields would be preserved as close to their wartime state as could be made possible. To indicate the thousands of soldiers and officers at the site during the battles, monuments and markers would show where a regiment was, where a prominent officer fell, and where a tactical maneuver had won or lost the battle.

The official dedications of both the Chickamauga and Chattanooga sites would be in September 1895, thirty-two years after the bloody battle of Chickamauga had been fought. Among those present were governors of fifteen states, nine

---

[1] Smith, *Golden Age of Battlefield Preservation*, 2.

senators, high-ranking members of the Army and Navy, and Vice President Adlai E. Stevenson. Over the next several years, other states, including Ohio, Kentucky, Florida, Pennsylvania, and New York, would arrange for monuments for their regiments and troops at Chickamauga. In 1899, at the dedication of the Indiana monuments, John T. Wilder, sixty-nine years of age, was called upon to give an address, and, on that occasion, he stood before them and relived the bloody, chaotic battle:

> My Dear Old Comrades—I bid you hail and welcome. It is now a whole generation since we were gathered here—thirty-two years. We fought over these slopes, where we did our best to sustain our country and our flag. We did not then stop to count odds. We "went in" wherever duty called, regardless of personal danger, to help settle forever the question of the division of this great country. You who have lived through the war, who have lived to see this great reunited country and meet here on this desperate battleground, have lived to see a spectacle no other nation and no other men have ever seen or experienced. Here, where two great armies fought and struggled for the supremacy for two long, bloody days, you behold tens of thousands of those combatants meeting to do honor and justice to all who were engaged in this great struggle. Honor to the living, justice to the dead. Here you have met in friendly intercourse many men who in that great battle you met in hottest combat; whose volleys you met with desolating fire; whose grand attack you met with rushing charge. How well do I remember your defense of the line of the Chickamauga River on that dusty Friday before the great battle was joined, when both armies were sweeping toward the goal of strife—Chattanooga. Your thin line opposed to two grand army corps, struggling to hold them back until "Thomas could come." How well you did your work and kept the Lafayette Road open and free for Thomas to throw the grand old Fourteenth Corps across the

front of Bragg's advance! How anxiously we waited that long, starless night at the forks of the road, a half-mile west of Viniard's repelling the enemy's attempt to seize that point, and how we felt when at 3 in the morning we heard the rumble of Thomas's march in our rear, closing in to meet the advance of Bragg the next day.

How well do I remember that bloody, desperate conflict at Viniard's all Saturday afternoon, when you swept the field with your repeaters; when Lilly treble-shotted his guns with canister! When we repulsed the charges that had made Sheridan, Davis and Wood stagger under their blows; when at night we thanked God that we held the ground we occupied in the morning; and then that long, bitter night, when every moment cries of pain and anguish went up from thousands of wounded whose forms dotted that desperate field; and then next morning, when we were withdrawn and placed "on the right fighting flank of the infantry line," just in rear and to the right of Glenn's house, how well you must remember that thirsty Sunday forenoon, when we lay on that dry hill, and when at 11 we saw the grand columns of Longstreet cross the Lafayette Road and sweep through the fields and woods toward our single line, and as heroic Sheridan was broken, we sprang to arms and swept in column down the hill and up the slope to Glenn's house and met the advance of Longstreet's left, first checking then breaking their column and driving their flank back through the woods to the Lafayette Road. We now stand on the very ground where the two lines first met. Yonder is the stump of the pine where gallant Colonel Funkhouser fell when leading his splendid charge of the Ninety-eight Illinois up the Glenn Hill. Yonder to the left is where brave Colonel A. O. Miller changed front under a rattling flank fire, and with his glorious Seventy-second Indiana drove back the force that had swept around our left flank and forced them off the hill northwardly from the Glenn house. Right here was the right of the One hundred and twenty-third Illinois which, under that splendid soldier, Colonel James Monroe, held back the fierce attempt to cut through our right center. Just where we stand the Seventeenth Indiana, under heroic Major William D. Jones, broke the left regiments of Longstreet's attack, capturing a number of prisoners and driving then rapidly eastward to the Lafayette Road. Just up there Captain Eli Lilly's Eighteenth Indiana Battery, with long-range canister, swept the ground in our front, firing rapidly over our heats. There, on the hill near the guns, was Colonel S.I. Atkins with his brave Ninety-second Illinois, repelling the attempt to swing round our rear and capture our battery and led horses. Oh, these were glorious moments—all our men engaged, repelling all attacks from every side, greatly outnumbered, but never outfought. I shall never forget the inspiring sight of Lilly's rush with his two guns, sweeping at a gallop down the slope and up Glenn's Hill, turning loose, almost before unlimbered, forty-pound canister straight into the teeth of the column that had just broken Lytle's line, and were in turn driven from our front by a fire no man could withstand. Now turn from scenes like these to the present, where a great nation, with its best representatives from the combatants of both sides, freely meet and mingle on their hallowed ground, eager to commemorate the grand homage and unselfish devotion here exhibited by Americans in defense of what they believed to be right. Where else on earth can such a spectacle be seen? The government has established a commission composed of one volunteer ex-Federal officer, one ex-Confederate officer, and one officer of the United States regular army, and a historian—all men of splendid character and integrity, all of whom were engaged in this great battle—who have charge of the ground and improvements, and all deeply impressed with their duty to history and to the living and the dead and to make this a just monument and record and an object-lesson of the bloodiest battle of our great war.

> Who of you that has survived that great conflict, who has lived through these desperate battles, does not feel a deeper interest in his country for this just recognition of his daring and his duty to his fellow men? Let us all more deeply resolve that our children shall be taught to forever maintain what we preserved in our day—a great, free and united country.

In August 1890, Union veteran General Abram O. Miller, a member of the Indiana 72nd Indiana Volunteer Infantry and the Lighting Brigade, proposed a brigade monument at the Chickamauga Military Park. Wilder, when contacted about this idea, wholeheartedly agreed and offered to personally match amounts raised by his brigade for the monument. The following year, at the brigade reunion at Worthington, Indiana, a monument organization was formed with General Miller as president and Wilder as treasurer. The organization was successful in raising money for a monument, which was decided to be a large tower, and construction began in the Chickamauga Military Park in spring 1892. Made from nearby Chickamauga limestone, the tower, which would become the largest monument on the battlefield, was placed on the site that General Rosecrans used as his quarters and where Sheridan's men gave way to Longstreet's charge. Designed by Henry Hargreaves, from Johnson City, Tennessee, and E. E. Betts of the United States Engineering Corps, the tower rises to a height of eighty-five feet, with a spiral staircase inside leading to an observation deck on top.

Sixty feet of the tower had been constructed when the banking failure of 1893 slowed the incoming funds. A Tennessee bank that held $1200 of monument funds failed and work stopped on the tower. For several years the tower stood partially built. In 1897, Wilder was visiting an Indiana businessman and monument builder, Arthur A. McKain, who, upon hearing Wilder's account of the tower in Chickamauga, wrote a check for $1200 to cover the amount lost from the Tennessee bank. Work resumed on the tower, and Wilder suggested the following year at a brigade reunion that they should hold a reunion the following year at Chickamauga to dedicate it, in anticipation of the tower being completed. The reunion was held, in September 1899, and the tower, standing its full eighty-five feet, was dedicated on 20 September. Union officer (and after the war an Illinois politician) James A. Connolly gave the dedicatory address. Wilder followed his address with the following speech:

> Mr. Chairman, Ladies and Gentlemen: I have the honor to say that these gray-headed men before you were the gallant young men of thirty-six years ago, who on this bloody battlefield bared their breasts to the storms of civil war, and on this spot met the brave men of Longstreet's Legions, and here broke the great charge that had driven the splendid men of Sheridan in confusion to the rear. In this place they were so fortunate as to break that magnificent line of battle and send the men of Longstreet's left back three-quarters of a mile and saved the men of McCook's gallant corps from further pursuit. Here in the presence of many who wore the gray on that fateful day, we can tell the truthful story of how Wilder's Brigade did their whole duty; of how they held Alexander's bridge on the 18th and kept Walker's corps from executing their purpose of throwing themselves across the LaFayette road in the rear of Rosecrans and between him army and Chattanooga. We can here tell how those gallant men held the cross roads at Hall's all night of the 18th in spite of the brave attempts of Bushrod Johnson to seize the LaFayette road at Viniard's. But we held them off until General George H. Thomas came up with his grand old 14th corps on the morning of the 19th and took position on the Chattanooga road to defend the move on Chattanooga. We

can here say that on the 19th the gallant Hood and Bushrod Johnson were repulsed by this Brigade at Viniard's, when they had broken Sheridan's division, and after they had broken the splendid attack of Davis' division this Brigade struck them in flank and compelled them to seek refuge in the woods east of Viniard's. We can also say that when Van-Cleve's division crossed the LaFayette road on that direful afternoon and were hurled back in confusion, we poured fire in their flank so terrible that even the splendid veterans of Hood were forced to yield the ground and return in hot haste to the cover of the woods. We can also say that when the gallant men of this Brigade met them with such a withering fire that they, too, were forced to give way and return to the woods from whence they came.

This command, composed of the 17th Indiana Infantry, Maj. William T. Jones commanding; the 72nd Indiana Infantry, Col. A. O. Miller commanding; the 92nd Illinois Infantry, Col. Smith D. Atkins commanding; the 98th Illinois Infantry, Col. J. J. Funkhouser commanding; the 123rd Illinois Infantry, Col. James Monroe commanding; and the 18th Indiana Battery, Capt. Eli Lilly commanding, all the infantry armed with Spencer repeating magazine rifles and aggregating about two thousand men in line, proved to the world that they could face the splendid veterans of Bragg's army; that they could successfully withstand Longstreet's Legions; that they trembled not when attacked by overwhelming force and all supports were gone. They proved their manhood by driving their attack with irresistible power and recovering the ground that even Sheridan had yielded to the bravest enemy that had ever fought on the bloodiest battlefields of Tennessee and Virginia.

This monument to their steadfast patriotism, their unyielding courage, was built by contributions from the gallant men who composed the Brigade. It stands on the spot where General Rosecrans' headquarters were on the 19th and forenoon of the 20th. It is erected in no vainglorious mood. It marks the line where the bravest of the brave Americans met in headlong conflict, each determined to win, and where the best armament proved successful. On this grand battlefield thousands died in defense of those principles that they had been trained to believe in, and which they thoroughly believed were right; where else on God's earth could such a conflict be carried to a close and find such results? These men were honorable Americans, and when the war was fought to a finish all agreed to live in peace, and have honestly kept their compact. No other people have done this in good faith. I thank God that I have lived to see the sons of these heroes from both sides join in the ranks of our country's defenders and under one common flag march to the tunes of "Dixie" and "Star Spangled Banner" with all the same light, springy step, the same patriotic impulse that impelled you men when you believed your duty was to follow and fight for the flags that waved over the proud hosts which joined battle on this bloody field. I am as proud of the memory of those who died under one flag as I am of those who fell under the other; both believed they were right; both died for the right as they saw it. We who fought for the stars and stripes give the hand of friendly fellowship to those who fought for the stars and bars. The sons of both sides have proved their readiness to march shoulder to shoulder to any part of the world where their common country calls and prove that their chief pride is in showing how the sons of the men of the great Civil War can best imitate the actions of their fathers. To you, General Boynton, as the representative of our great country, I have the honor of turning over the custody of this monument. May it stand for ages to show the coming generations how their ancestors fought for their principles. It stands as a monument to the valor of those who fought on both sides. May its lessons be learned by all our descendants.

Other addresses were given by Henry V. Boynton, Captain William Rule (a Tennessee newspaper publisher who had fought for the Union during the war), Colonel Tomlinson Fort (a local Confederate veteran), General Smith D. Atkins, and Indiana governor James A. Mount, who had served under Wilder as a member of the 72nd Indiana Infantry.

Throughout his life, John Wilder often had many pans in the fire. In 1889 Wilder and his wife, Martha, had bought a house in Johnson City, Tennessee, in order for him to better manage the 3-Cs railroad as the vice president. This home brought him back near the region where he had built his Cloudland Hotel on Roan Mountain in northeast Tennessee and had other mining interests. Johnson City is in northeast Tennessee and sits where three Tennessee counties, Carter, Washington, and Sullivan, meet. Named for Henry Johnson, a businessman who first settled the area around 1856 and built the first train depot, Johnson City became a hub for railroads in the southeastern part of the United States. Interested in expanding into other business ventures in addition to the railroads, Wilder developed and built the Carnegie Land Company, the Carnegie Furnace, and the Carnegie Hotel, all in Johnson City. The fact that the name of Carnegie, obviously for American industrialist and philanthropist Andrew Carnegie, was put to many of Wilder's projects points to some connection between Carnegie and either Johnson City or Wilder himself. There is no known relationship between the two industrialists, but stories can be found that Carnegie was willing to build libraries, foundries, and other businesses in Johnson City, contingent on the town being renamed "Carnegie." Apparently, this offer was not taken up by the city directors, but Wilder may have been attempting to curry favor with Carnegie to encourage the industrialist to invest in the town anyway. It does not appear the plan worked. Wilder also set up a small lumber mill in Chestoa, Tennessee, south of Johnson City, in Unicoi County. Wilder's popularity was evident in Johnson City, as was his wife's, as they lived there while he started and conducted his businesses. The town would honor Martha by opening a local public school and naming it the Martha Wilder School.

Johnson City was a growing town, but in 1880 had a population of just under nine hundred residents. By 1890, the population had grown to more than forty-six hunred due to the rise of industry, and the East Tennessee and Western North Carolina Railway was part of that growth as well. The East Tennessee and Western North Carolina Railway had been established several decades earlier to move ore to furnaces in Johnson City. By 1881 the line extended from the Cranberry Mines in North Carolina to Johnson City, Tennessee, cutting through the mountains and gorges. Wilder opened the Carnegie Iron Company in Johnson City in 1892, a blast furnace capable of producing an annual output of thirty-six thousand pounds of pig iron. The furnace used magnetite ore from the Cranberry Mines, thirty miles to the east. This mill would be short-lived, as the stock market crash of 1893 resulted in the company's insolvency.[2]

There's an interesting anecdote in Williams's biography of Wilder that likely happened during this time. Williams tells of an occasion when Great Britain's Duke of Marlborough was touring the area. Wilder allegedly gave the duke a tour of his mines in Cranberry, North Carolina, and when the duke asked how far the vein of ore extended, Wilder is said to have replied, "the devil is now making iron from the bottom of it."[3] Exactly

[2] Chamberlain, *Family Chronicle*, 25.
[3] Williams, *Wilder*, 43.

when this occurred is not known, but the British publication, the *Fortnightly Review* included in its April 1891 issue the article "Virginia Mines and American Rails," written by the Duke of Marlborough after a recent American tour. This particular Duke of Marlborough would have been George Charles Spencer-Churchill, the eighth Duke of Marlborough and an uncle of Winston Churchill. The period also coincides with the time in which Wilder was in Johnson City, which is close to Virginia, and involved with mines in the area, so it's quite likely it occurred during this time.

An unfortunate recession and economic panic in 1893 would have an impact on Wilder. The Panic of 1893 was a financial disaster brought about by a recession in England that had begun three years earlier. This recession resulted in the failure of the Baring Brothers Bank, the British bank that had been a primary player in the collaboration between British investors and American businessmen and industrialists, including Wilder. Even though the Bank of England came to the rescue of Baring Brothers, what resulted was an export of $68 million in gold from the United States to Europe, as nervous English investors liquidated their stock holdings in American companies. This caused a drop in the gold reserve below $100 million, which was considered the minimum safe level by the US government. As this reserve was seen as being in jeopardy, the value of and confidence in the American dollar sank. Stock prices plunged as investors, in 1893, quickly sold stocks and other investments, sending the New York Stock Exchange stock prices downward. Banks in the South saw a rush of customers panicking and taking their money out. Businesses were hit hard, with many failing over the panic, and a three-year economic depression followed in the United States. Wilder, like many other capitalists, suffered financially, and although the exact amount of Wilder's losses is unknown, it has been reported to have been as high as $750,000. Nevertheless, at sixty-three years of age, Wilder still had visions, ideas, and expertise, and he did what he did best, which was to move to newer ventures and enterprises.

To add to Wilder's woes in 1893, Martha Wilder died in Johnson City from cancer, having suffered from it for several years. For years she had stood quietly by her husband, kept the home, raised the children, nursed him when his illness brought him home from the war for recovery, and supported him through all his postwar businesses and travels. Her body was brought back to Chattanooga, and she was buried in the Forrest Hills Cemetery at the foot of Lookout Mountain, in a growing Wilder family plot that also served as the resting place for Wilder's parents.

Chapter 10

Back to the Mines, Continued Service, and the Final Years

In 1895, John Wilder began visiting the small town of Monterey, Tennessee, in Putnam County. Forty-five miles northwest of Rockwood where Wilder had several decades before established the Roane Iron Company, Monterey and the area immediately north of it showed promise and potential for mining ventures. In addition, Wilder was also attracted to the area by the Nashville-Knoxville Railroad, which had a line running from Cookeville to Monterey. This railroad, Wilder knew, would be beneficial to any mines in the area. Additional railway expansion was expected as there were plans to add rail lines to the several mining communities further north in Fentress County. Wilder opened a small coal mine in Mineral Springs, a small village close to Monterey, and was able to move the coal produced there via the railroad to Monterey.[1]

In 1901 Wilder, now seventy-one years of age, brought two carpenters, William Livingstone and Parris Shallows, to an area twenty miles northeast of Monterey, in order to lay out a small town where he was developing a mine.[2] This area was remote and hilly, heavily wooded, and with deep ravines. Wilder had discovered the area had a rich coal seam, and he secured backing for this venture from residents in the town of Jamestown, to the north.[3] There had already been a lumber mill in the area, and the local residents called their new settlement

---

[1] Duke, *Coal Mining, Railroading & Logging*, 19.

[2] Ibid., 25.

[3] *History of Fentress County*, 49–50.

Hightown. A boarding house was in operation in the area, and Wilder was a frequent visitor as he continued to explore the area. The town was developed, as was the mine, and was given the name of Wilder, but only after mail began showing up there addressed as such.

The following year, 1902, Wilder opened the Fentress Coal & Coke Mine Number 1 in the town of Wilder. A rail line would follow the next year, linking the towns of Wilder and Monterey, approximately fifteen miles apart. The town of Wilder grew, and houses for the miners and their families were constructed. Wilder had schools built for the town's children as well as a church. In a period of ten years, the town grew to include not just a school and church, but a hotel, train depot, post office, doctor's office, and a population of over two thousand. By the early 1920s, more than five hundred workers were on the payroll, and the town of Wilder would ultimately have four separate mines.[4] Other developers established mines in the area, including one in Davidson, just a few miles to the north. The small towns and mines would survive for a while, even after Wilder's death. After strikes in 1924 and again in 1932 (this strike even resulting in violence), the mines operated through World War II. They carried on for a few more decades after the war but began playing out and closing down by the 1960s. Today, the town of Wilder has returned to nature; only a few houses of a more recent construction are in the area. Gone are the miners' shacks, stores, and other buildings, and the remote area is overgrown and heavily wooded. Both the Wilder and Davidson cemeteries are still accessible and are the few signs that towns were once there. Today, there is little evidence of the mines, or settlements, in Wilder or Davidson.

[4] Wheeler, *History of Wilder, Davidson, Highland Junction, Sandy, and "The Hollow,"* 17.

Driving through the area, one would be unaware that towns there ever existed.

In 1897, President William McKinley appointed John Wilder to the position of pension agent in Knoxville. The government had been issuing pensions to war veterans since the Revolutionary War, at first to veterans injured during the war, their widows, and to veterans who were living in extreme poverty. These pensions continued after the Civil War, but, in the early 1890s, the Dependent Pension Act was passed that enabled any veteran to qualify if he became disabled at any time. By 1906, old age was considered enough of a disability to qualify. Wilder's role as pension agent was to oversee the thousands of dollars distributed to Knoxville-area pension recipients, and he investigated claims as necessary. Wilder had assistance in obtaining the position from former president Benjamin Harrison. Acquainted with each other, and possibly friends, they likely had met during the Civil War since they were both Indiana officers serving in the Army of the Cumberland. Samuel Cole Williams's 1936 biography on Wilder alludes to a favor Wilder bestowed on Benjamin Harrison in May 1878 that was "too intimate a nature for recital" to be described in more detail. Williams goes no further in explaining what the situation or favor was, but in May 1878, Harrison's father, John Scott Harrison—the only man in American history to have been both the son of a president (William Henry Harrison) and the father of another (Benjamin Harrison)—passed away unexpectedly. After Harrison's funeral, the family arrived at the family plot at the Congress Green Cemetery in North Bend, Ohio. It was there they discovered that the gravesite of another family member who had died just a short period before had been disturbed. In fact, his body was missing, evidently the work of grave-robbers. Fearing a similar fate for John Scott

Harrison, the family hired a guard to watch the burial site, lest it be robbed as well, and went in search of the missing relative's body. This was during a time when grave-robbing was not an uncommon method for medical schools to acquire cadavers for their students. A couple of days later the family got a tip that an unidentified body had recently been received at the local medical school. Upon a search, they found hidden in a shaft a shrouded body hanging by the neck. Pulling it up, and expecting to find the younger relative's body, they were shocked to find the body of John Scott Harrison! Apparently, the guard who was watching over his grave assumed the grave-robbers would not be so bold as to return to the scene of their recent crime so soon, so he had made only sporadic check-ups. John Scott Harrison was buried again, the perpetrators found and arrested, and several weeks later they found the body of the younger relative, which by then had made its way to a medical school in Ann Arbor, Michigan. What role Wilder might have played in this episode is not known, but this might have been the incident Williams refers to. At one point during this unfortunate episode, the citizens of Lawrenceburg, Indiana, only ten miles from North Bend, Ohio, approached the Harrison family to offer their cemetery for re-interring former president William Henry Harrison's remains, which were also at the Congress Green Cemetery in North Bend. They did this on the assumption that the family might not want to keep the family plot at that cemetery. This offer was declined.[5] Wilder had a connection with Lawrenceburg, having had a foundry there in the early 1850s, so it's possible he had been involved somehow with this offer.

Perhaps it was being around his fellow Civil War officers and soldiers and the activities surrounding the organization of

[5] Sievers, *Harrison Horror*, 1–33.

the national battleground parks and reunions that drove Wilder to inquire about a commission during the Spanish-American War in 1898. The United States was once again engaged in a war, this time with Spain, and soldiers from the South and North were fighting under the same flag for the first time since the Civil War had ended. The United States government gave commissions to three former Confederate generals, perhaps to boost morale of soldiers from the South. Joseph Wheeler, Fitzhugh Lee (nephew of Robert E. Lee), and Thomas Rosser were given commissions although only General Wheeler would lead troops in any action. "Fightin' Joe Wheeler," as he was known, was a native of Georgia, a West Point alumnus, and had been an officer in the Confederate Army of Tennessee. After the war, he had served in the US House of Representatives from the 8th district of Alabama. He not only served in the Spanish-American War (even overseeing Teddy Roosevelt's Rough Riders) but also saw service in the Philippine-American War that followed. Upon his death in 1906, he became one of only a few former Confederate officers to be buried in Arlington National Cemetery.

Wilder, at sixty-eight years of age, made overtures to the government for a commission as well, but the government declined. However, in June 1898, Wilder did arrange for the military to establish a camp in Knoxville to house and quarter soldiers of the 6th US Volunteer Infantry prior to their being sent to fight in Cuba. This fort was named Camp Wilder, and it was in service only one month. But in that time, nearly one thousand soldiers from Tennessee, Kentucky, and Ohio were billeted there. The camp was commanded by Colonel Lawrence Davis Tyson, a West Point graduate. By the end of July 1898, Camp Wilder was dismantled, and the soldiers and officers were sent to Camp George H. Thomas in north Georgia, near the Chickamauga battleground.[6] In an interview printed in the *Wilmington (NC) Semi-Weekly Messenger*, Wilder suggested that the government raise one hundred thousand Black troops and put them under the command of General Fitzhugh Lee for the purpose of capturing Cuba—and then the Caribbean island could be "turned over to the negro."[7]

In order to better conduct his obligations as pension agent in Knoxville, Wilder bought a small farm on the outskirts of the town and moved there, despite operating several mines in north Tennessee that would need his attention. Wilder would be reappointed pension agent by President Theodore Roosevelt in 1901 and again in 1909 by President William Howard Taft. During his years in Knoxville, Wilder continued to be active and helped organize the Knoxville Power Company in 1900, serving as vice president of the company as well as on the board of directors. He was also involved in developing the company's first hydroelectric power plant.[8] When the Pension Agent office was relocated to Washington, D.C., Wilder retired and returned to his home in Monterey to enjoy his final years.

In 1903, General Wilder was as widely popular in Monterey as he was everywhere else he had lived. In the fall of that year, students from Monterey High School attended a program in the city park, in which the seventy-three-year-old Wilder regaled the students with stories of the Civil War and his life.[9] Ever the entrepreneur, Wilder still had the energy to build a home, a stable, and another hotel, all in Monterey. This hotel, which opened in 1908, was called the Imperial Hotel and would operate as a hotel until the early 1970s. When it was

[6] Now Fort Oglethorpe, Georgia.
[7] *Wilmington (NC) Semi-Weekly Messenger*, 1 April 1898.
[8] Stahl, *Greater Johnson City*, 68.
[9] Dillard, *Standing Stone, Tenn.*, 153.

built, it was said to have been the grandest hotel between Nashville and Knoxville, with eighty rooms and running water.[10]

In the early 1900s, Wilder's health began to deteriorate though he was still quite active with his business ventures. Wilder, throughout his adult life, did not use tobacco of any kind and did not drink alcohol. However, he was said to have a voracious appetite, which resulted in his gaining considerable weight in his later years. Still occasionally suffering from illnesses he developed during the war years, he was hospitalized in Knoxville in 1904. He was assigned a personal nurse, a woman in her mid-twenties named Dora Ethel Lee. She was an alumna of Asheville Female College, in North Carolina, and had lived and worked in Indianapolis as a nurse, taking classes at the Medical College of Indiana in Indianapolis. She was also said to be distantly related to Robert E. Lee. Despite the age difference of approximately five decades, a relationship developed, and they married in Lake Toxaway, North Carolina, after a brief courtship.[11] Area newspapers reported the wedding as "secret" and gave the bride's age as eighteen and Wilder's as eighty (they were, in fact, twenty-eight and seventy-four, respectively). As a wedding gift, Wilder gave Dora the title to his Knoxville farm. They lived briefly in Indianapolis in 1905 in order for her to continue her medical studies, which Wilder financed, and then they moved back to Knoxville. Dora Lee Wilder became one of the earliest female students at the Tennessee Medical College, receiving her degree in 1906.[12] Wilder

---

[10] World War I hero and Tennessean, Alvin C. York, even stayed at the Imperial Hotel in the early 1950s.

[11] Wilder would not be the only aging Civil War veteran to marry a much younger woman, as this was not entirely uncommon in the early 1900s.

[12] Dickinson, "Dr. Dora Lee Wilder," 75.

suffered health problems again in 1907 and traveled to the Mayo Clinic in Rochester, Minnesota, for an undisclosed operation. That same year, he ran for the position of commander in chief of the Grand Army of the Republic but was not elected.

Upon resigning his position as pension agent in 1910, Wilder and his young wife moved to Monterey, where Wilder occupied himself by overseeing the construction of the Imperial Hotel.[13] Dora Wilder worked as a physician briefly in Monterey before giving up the practice. That year, Jacob M. Dickinson, United States secretary of war, appointed Wilder to be the secretary of the Shiloh Commission, an administrative agency overseeing the battlefield in western Tennessee. Wilder had not participated in the famed battle in spring 1862 but had arrived on the scene shortly after it was over and observed the carnage. This appointment would only last a year. The following year, 1911, the eighty-one-year-old Wilder was appointed the commissioner of the Chickamauga and Chattanooga Military Park, where he had been involved in its development as a national military park two decades earlier. Wilder held this position until his death six years later.

In 1912, Wilder was still popular in Chattanooga, and an article in the *Chattanooga Times* reported that Wilder had recently purchased land on Walden's Ridge (today's town of Signal Mountain), a mountain ridge just north of Chattanooga. Wilder intended to build a home there, the article stated, in an area where he had placed a signal corps during the war and which had since been known as Wilder's Point. The house would have, the article went on, eleven rooms and would be "a seventy-eight foot square building," at a cost of $23,000. His vast military collection, as well as his geological collections of

[13] Upon Wilder's death in 1917, the hotel became the property of Dora Wilder.

minerals, would be kept at this home. Perhaps it was Wilder's intent to live out his life there, near Chattanooga. If the house was ever built, and no records have been found to suggest it was, it apparently didn't stand for long.[14]

In 1915, Anne Bachman Hyde, Chattanooga historian and historian-general of the United Daughters of the Confederacy, ran into Wilder at the Read House, a popular hotel in Chattanooga. She knew Wilder and had been lifelong friends with one of Wilder's daughters. Hyde's father, the Reverend Jonathan Waverly Bachman, was also a close friend of Wilder. The Reverend Bachman, a lifelong Tennessean known as "Chattanooga's Pastor," had been a Confederate Presbyterian chaplain during the war and in his later years was the chaplain-general of the United Confederate Veterans.

Wanting to set the record straight on a Civil War matter, Mrs. Hyde asked Wilder if he had deliberately targeted the Presbyterian church when he led Union troops into Chattanooga in summer 1863. The church had been damaged by cannonballs after troops shelled the city from nearby Cameron Hill as an announcement of their arrival. Wilder, who loved to talk about the war, told her, "Annie, you know that I would never fire at your Pa's church [Wilder evidently thought that it already was Bachman's church, which it wouldn't be until several years after the war]. I was trying to get the range of the *Chattanooga Rebel*, published by Henry Watterson across Market Street, and it was hard to get at." The *Chattanooga Rebel* had been a popular local Civil War-era newspaper during the war, and it was known to publish troop movements and other

---

14 "Wilder Point for a Home," *Chattanooga Times*, 12 May 1912. A descendent of Wilder did tell the author that the house burned down, along with his military memorabilia and collections. The date of this fire is unknown.

information neither side particularly wanted revealed. It was also during this conversation that Wilder expressed his opinion of General William T. Sherman. "Sherman knew it all," Wilder said sarcastically of his superior officer. He continued,

> You could never tell him anything. When he decided to cross the river and go down the north end of Missionary Ridge, I told him to be careful, that there was a depression there and he might find some Rebels. He said, 'No, he had all the maps and there was no gap 'til Rossville.' I said, well go on, which he did and when he reached the gap there he met Gen. Pat Cleburne with the disastrous results the world knows.[15]

This recollection apparently was a reference to Sherman's troops being rebuffed by Patrick Cleburne's smaller division during the battle of Missionary Ridge.

In 1915, having turned eighty-five years old, Wilder began spending the winter in Jacksonville, Florida, preferring the milder climate to that of Monterey, Tennessee. On 20 October 1917, only a few weeks after arriving at Jacksonville for the season, Wilder died at the age of eighty-seven. Senility and bronchitis are the reasons for death listed on his death certificate. Two of his daughters, now adults, and Dora were at his side when he passed away early in the morning. Two weeks earlier, he had stopped at Chattanooga along his route to Florida in what would be his final visit. His funeral in Chattanooga was conducted by Reverend Jonathan Waverly Bachman. Despite having fought on opposite sides of the Civil War, the two had been friends for many years, and Bachman had agreed years earlier to conduct Wilder's funeral should Wilder precede him in death. Reverend Bachman stated at the funeral,

---

[15] Mynders, "Next to the News," *Chattanooga Times*, 1 July 1956.

> The world is poorer since General Wilder died. He made the world brighter and happier while he lived in it. It used to be said of this man that he was visionary. So he was. He was a seer. In his citizenship, like the soldier, he was in the front rank in all good works. He was devoted to the welfare of Chattanooga and this section. His brain and his heart were at the service of the people. He loved his fellow man. This was his town and this was his country and his people.

Wilder was laid to rest next to his first wife, Martha, and next to his parents in the family plot at the Forest Hills Cemetery in St. Elmo, a small Chattanooga community at the foot of Lookout Mountain.

Even though Wilder had not resided in Chattanooga for quite some time, the local newspaper ran his obituary on the front page, the headline reading, "Death Calls General Wilder."

After Wilder's death, his holdings were sold off over a five-year period by his son, Stuart Wilder, and his son-in-law Francis A. Stratton (married to Wilder's daughter, Edith), who both served as executors of Wilder's estate. The proceeds were divided in seven equal parts and distributed to Wilder's six children and to his second wife, Dora Lee Wilder. He bequeathed his son, Stuart, his commission as brigadier-general in the United States Army; his daughter Rachel received his commission as colonel, and his daughter Edith received his commission as captain, as well as a solid set of silver he had purchased during a trip to England. In addition to the farm, he gave Dora a silver loving cup. His daughter Mary received his mineral and fossil collections, as well as military papers, books, and heirlooms. His grandson, Wilder Stratton, received his commission of lieutenant colonel.[16]

In the year that Wilder died, 33,092 other Civil War Union veterans also died, forty-two years after the war had ended. By then, animosities were mostly forgotten. The year before had seen approximately thirty-four thousand Union veterans die, as calculated through pension rolls. After 1917, the numbers started going down each year until the 1950s when the last Civil War veterans passed away.[17] However, starting in April 1917, the United States would produce more war veterans as the nation entered a new war, a war that had been waging in Europe for three years and would quickly be known as "The Great War," and later as World War I.

After Wilder's death, Dora Lee Wilder, who was forty-two years of age when her husband died, married Percy Berkley Smith, who worked for the Tennessee Central Railroad. Although both a nurse and a doctor, she had quit practicing medicine shortly after marrying Wilder in 1904. Percy Berkley Smith had been friends with the Wilders, having met them while staying in the Imperial Hotel in Monterey. Smith had served as a pallbearer at Wilder's funeral. Dora Lee Wilder Smith lived until 1963, even outliving her second husband, who passed away in 1959. Dora and her second husband are both buried in Alexander, North Carolina, her childhood home. Wilder's children, five daughters and one son, all lived to adulthood. His son, Stuart, carried on the family name, but three of John Wilder's daughters, Mary, Anna, and Martha, never married. Stuart outlived his sisters and died in Newtown,

---

[16] "General John T. Wilder's Will Expresses Touching Sentiment," *Chattanooga Times*, 23 October 1917.

[17] Myers and Shudde, "Mortality Experience of Union Civil War Veterans," 65.

Connecticut, in 1963. In his adult life he had been a vice president with the Westchester Lighting Company in New York. Edith Wilder had married Arthur Hoyt Scott, son of the founder of the Scott Paper Company, and had traveled the world with her husband.

The John T. Wilder legacy lives on as well. The Wilder Tower, eighty-five feet tall, still stands in the Chickamauga and Chattanooga National Military Park, which memorializes one of the Civil War's bloodiest and biggest battles. Many of his soldiers during the war took such pride at being under Wilder's command that they requested their membership in "Wilder's Lightning Brigade" noted on their tombstones.

John Thomas Wilder lived by the creed that necessity is the mother of invention. Throughout his life and work, he determined what obstacles were in his way, and he found a way to resolve them. Whether it was going to a fellow officer and gentleman on the other side to ask for advice, or to invent a machine or tool he needed to accomplish a task, he took resourcefulness to a higher level than most. When he lost a fortune in the panic of 1893, he continued developing his enterprises and forging ahead, much as he did at Hoover's Gap, Tennessee, in 1863. There was no stopping him. Apprentice, millwright, husband and father, soldier and officer, mayor, postmaster, hotelier, and entrepreneur, John T. Wilder left a mark in many fields during his life and in so doing etched his name in American history.

Acknowledgments

Writing *John T. Wilder* took a bit longer than I anticipated when I began the project. Between starting it and publishing it, I published two other books, one as editor and the other as a co-author. I put *John T. Wilder* aside for periods of time, twice for nearly a full year, but I never gave up on it. Now that it's finished, I can look back, acknowledge and thank those who were especially helpful and supportive in seeing this project through. *John T. Wilder* may not have been written had it not been for the encouragement and support given me by two eminent historians in Chattanooga, Tennessee. Dr. James Livingood, longtime history professor at the University of Tennessee at Chattanooga, was likely a key figure in the university obtaining the collection of John T. Wilder letters and documents, donated by one of Wilder's daughters in the early 1960s. Shortly before Dr. Livingood passed away, I was able to discuss this project with him, and he expressed the need for a new biography of Wilder. Historian Nathaniel Cheairs Hughes, Jr.—Nat Hughes—was also supportive. He gave me the gentle shove I needed to begin the project and provided much-needed advice early on. Sadly, both of these historians are no longer with us, and I would certainly have benefited from their kind advice and support during the writing of this book.

Others have been helpful while I was researching and writing this book. Jim Ogden, historian of the Chickamauga and Chattanooga National Military Park, was a tremendous help with his support and encyclopedic knowledge of Civil War matters in southeastern Tennessee and northern Georgia and of Civil War history in general. Descendants of John T. Wilder, notably Tom Maher, Becky Everett, and Mary Harrell-Sesniak, were also supportive and helpful, particularly in their allowing use of family photographs of Wilder. The staff at the Archives of Appalachia at East Tennessee State University were helpful in providing a picture of Wilder's Cloudland Hotel and also provided information about Wilder's time in eastern Tennessee. Russell Wilhoite, historian in Greensburg, Indiana, was also helpful in providing information about Wilder in Greensburg. The staff at Tennessee Tech University graciously allowed me to use a photo of Dora Lee Wilder, John T. Wilder's second wife. The staff at the Tennessee State Library and Archives were helpful in allowing a picture of Wilder's Roane Iron Company to be used.

I am indebted to editorial work by my brother, Bob Cox, whose historical knowledge and keen eye for clarity and description were invaluable; he corrected errors and supplied important information to further explain several matters. Research assistance by Georgia Cravey was also helpful. Support by historians Chris Childers, Tim Ezzell, Maury Nicely, and Aaron Purcell proved to be extremely helpful in bringing this book to publication. I am also deeply grateful for the support from the Mercer University Press's editor, Marc Jolley, for his interest in and support of this manuscript, for accepting it for publication, as well as for the staff's preparing it for publication.

Most importantly, I am grateful to my wife, Dianne, who indulged and accompanied me on various research trips throughout the eastern United States. She has seen this project through from beginning to end. All my love and gratitude for her support.

Bibliography

PRIMARY SOURCES

Manuscripts, Interviews, and Government Records

Archives of Appalachia, East Tennessee State University, Johnson City

Roan Mountain Project Collection 1991–1992, Acc. 435.

Oral Histories

Julian Caldwell, transcript, box 1, folder 3

Plato Garland, transcript, box 1, folder 4

Harry Heaton, transcript, box 1, folder 5

The Ron D. Vance and Barbara H. Wickersham Collection, Acc. 621.

Articles and Interview Transcriptions

Florine Garland and Mary Gree, box 3, folder 9

Jeter Goudge, box 3, folder 13

Margaret Propst and Florence Graybeal, box 3, folder 14

Noble and Lois Jones, box 4, folder 1

Ed and Makie Street, box 5, folder 1

Mae Street, box 5, folder 5

The Murrell Family Collection, Acc. 432.

University of Tennessee at Chattanooga, Special Collections & University Archives

Chamberlain, Morrow. *A Family Chronicle.* Unpublished ms. 1931.

John T. Wilder Papers, MSS 001.

Indiana State Library, Indianapolis

John T. Wilder Papers, Manuscript Section, Indiana State Library, Indianapolis

Regimental Correspondence, 17th Indiana Volunteers, Indiana State Archives

Greensburg—Decatur County Public Library [Indiana]

John T. Wilder Collection

National Archives, Washington, D.C.
Compiled Records Showing Service of Military Units in Volunteer Union Organizations. Fourteenth Infantry through Nineteenth Infantry [Illinois and Indiana]. Microfilm Rolls 29 and 38.
United States War Department. *The War of the Rebellion: A Compilation of the Official Records of the United and Confederate Armies.* 70 vols. In 218 parts and index. Washington, D.C.: Government Printing Office, 1880–1901. Cited as *OR.*

SECONDARY SOURCES

American Institute of Mining Engineers. "New Patents." *Engineering and Mining Journal* 27 (January–June 1879): 242.
Andrews, Garnett. "A Battle Planned, but Not Fought." *Confederate Veteran* 5/6 (June 1897): 293–95.
Armstrong, Zella. *The History of Hamilton County and Chattanooga.* Chattanooga, TN: Lookout Publishing Company, 1931.
Ashdown, Paul, and Edward Caudill. *The Myth of Nathan Bedford Forrest.* Lanham, MD: Rowman & Littlefield Publishers, 2005.
Barnhart, John D. "The Impact of the Civil War on Indiana." *Indiana Magazine of History* 57/3 (September 1961): 185–224.
Baumgartner, Richard A. *Blue Lightning: Wilder's Mounted Infantry Brigade in the Battle of Chickamauga.* Huntington, WV: Blue Acorn Press, 2007.
Beers, J. B. *History of Greene County, New York, with Biographical Sketches of its Prominent Men.* Cornwallville, NY: Hope Farm Press, 1969.
Belissary, Constantine G. "The Rise of Industry and the Industrial Spirit in Tennessee, 1865–1885." *Journal of Southern History* 19/2 (May 1953): 194–97.
Benefiel, W. H. H. *Souvenir: The Seventeenth Indiana Regiment.* Pendleton, IN: self-published, 1913.
Benhart, John E., Jr. *Appalachian Aspirations.* Knoxville: University of Tennessee Press, 2007.

Brown, Kent Masterson. "Munfordville: The Campaign and Battle along Kentucky's Strategic Axis." *Register of the Kentucky Historical Society* 97/3 (Summer 1999): 265–73.

Bruce, Robert C. *Lincoln and the Tools of War*. Urbana: University of Illinois Press, 1989.

Bulla, David W. *Lincoln's Censor: Milo Hascall and the Freedom of the Press in Civil War Indiana*. West Lafayette, IN: Purdue University Press, 2009.

Chandler, Alfred D., Jr. "Anthracite Coal and the Beginnings of the Industrial Revolution in the United States." *Business History Review* 46/2 (Summer 1972): 141–81.

Chapman, Ashton. "Former Clerk Recalls Proud Cloudland Hotel atop Roan." *Charlotte Observer*, 8 July 1953.

Chattanooga News, 20 October 1917.

Chattanooga Times, 12 May 1912 and 21 October 1917.

"Cloudland Hotel...Only Memories Remain." *Elizabethton (TN) Star*, 18 June 1995.

"Col. John A. Washington, C.S.A." *Confederate Veteran* 30/7 (July 1922): 245–46.

Congressional Quarterly's Guide to U.S. Elections. Washington D.C.: CQ Press, 2010.

Connolly, James A. *Three Years in the Army of the Cumberland*. Bloomington: Indiana University Press, 1959.

Daniel, Larry J. *Days of Glory: The Army of the Cumberland*. Baton Rouge: Louisiana State University Press, 2004.

Dickinson, W. Calvin. "Dr. Dora Lee Wilder: Pioneer Female Physician of the Cumberland Plateau." *Journal of East Tennessee History* 83 (2011): 72–79.

Dillard, John R. "John T. Wilder—The Soldier." *Catamount* 8/2 (September 1984): 1–4B.

———. *Standing Stone, Tenn.: Monterey: Early History*. Nashville: Harris Press, 1989.

Doster, James F. "The Chattanooga Rolling Mill: An Industrial By-Product of the Civil War." *East Tennessee Historical Society's Publication* 36 (1964): 45–55.

Duke, Jason. *Tennessee: Coal Mining, Railroading & Logging in Cumberland, Fentress, Overton, and Putnam Counties.* Paducah, KY: Turner Publishing Company, 2003.

Edwards, William B. *Civil War Guns.* Harrisburg, PA: Stackpole Company, 1962.

Eller, Ronald D. *Miners, Millhands, and Mountaineers: Industrialization of the Appalachian South, 1880–1930.* Knoxville: University of Tennessee Press, 1982.

Engerud, Hal. *The History of the Siege of Munfordville.* Louisville: Civil War Round Table, 1962.

Engle, Stephen D. *Don Carlos Buell: Most Promising of All.* Chapel Hill: University of North Carolina Press, 1999.

Engle, Stephen D. *Struggle for the Heartland.* Lincoln: University of Nebraska Press, 2001.

Ezzell, Tim. *Chattanooga, 1865–1900: A City Set Down in Dixie.* Knoxville: University of Tennessee Press, 2014.

Findling, John E. *Historical Dictionary of World's Fairs and Expositions, 1851–1988.* New York: Greenwood Press, 1990.

Fitch, John. *Annals of the Army of the Cumberland.* Philadelphia: J. B. Lippincott & Co., 1864.

Frazer, John F., ed. "American Patents which issued in October, 1859." *Journal of the Franklin Institute of the State of Pennsylvania, for the Promotion of the Mechanic Arts.* 3rd ser. 39/1 (whole 69/409) (January 1860): 35 (#248).

"General John T. Wilder's Will Expresses Touching Sentiment." *Chattanooga News,* 23 October 1917, 13.

Goforth, James A. *Building the Clinchfield: A Construction History of America's Most Unusual Railroad.* Erwin, TN: Gem Publishers, 1989.

Govan, Gilbert E., and James W. Livingood. *The Chattanooga Country, 1540–1976.* Knoxville: University of Tennessee Press, 1977.

———. *The University of Chattanooga: Sixty Years.* Kingsport, TN: Kingsport Press, 1947.

Hall, Jere, and Jack B. Shelley, eds. *Valley of Challenge and Change: Roane County, Tennessee, 1860–1900.* Johnson City: East Tennessee Historical Society, 1986.

Harbison, Robert E. "Wilder's Brigade in the Tullahoma and Chattanooga Campaigns of the American Civil War." Master's thesis, U.S. Army Command and General Staff College, 2002.

Hardee, William J. *Rifle and Light Infantry Tactics for the Exercise and Manoeuvres of Troops When Acting as Light Infantry or Riflemen.* Philadelphia: Lippincott, Grambo & Co., 1855.

Harrison, Lowell H. *The Civil War in Kentucky.* Lexington: University Press of Kentucky, 1975.

———. "The Battle of Munfordville." *Civil War Times Illustrated* 13/3 (June 1974): 4–9; 45–47.

Heidler, David S., and Jeanne T. Heidler. *Encyclopedia of the Civil War: A Political, Social, and Military History.* Volume 1. Santa Barbara, CA: ABC-Clio, 2000.

Hicken, Victor. *Illinois in the Civil War.* Urbana: University of Illinois Press, 1991.

High, Edwin. *History of the Sixty-Eighth Regiment, Indiana Volunteer Infantry, 1862–1865.* Metamora, IN: Sixty-Eighth Indiana Infantry Association, 1902.

History of Fentress County, TN. Jamestown, TN: Fentress County Historical Society, 1987.

History of Tennessee. Nashville: Goodspeed Publishing Co., 1887.

Horn, Stanley F., ed. *Tennessee's War: 1861–1865. Described by Participants.* Nashville: Tennessee Civil War Centennial Commission, 1965.

House Journal of the First Session: Forty-First General Assembly of the State of Tennessee, which Convened at Nashville, on the First Monday in January, 1879. Nashville: American Steam Book and Job Office, 1879.

Hunter, Robert, and W. H. Chamberlin, eds. *Sketches of War History. 1861–1865: Papers Read Before the Ohio Commandery of the Military Order of the Loyal Legion of the United States.* Cincinnati: Monfort & Company, 1908.

Joslin, Michael. "Mine Provides Glimpse of Past." *Johnson City Press*, 26 January 1986, 3.

Kilborn, Lawson S. *Dedication of the Wilder Brigade Monument on Chickamauga Battlefield on the Thirty-Sixth Anniversary of the Battle, September 20, 1899.* Marshall, IL: The Herald Press, 1900.

Kivette, Everett M. "A Very Special Mountain." *The State* 39/23 (May 1972): 14–16.

Knoxville Daily Chronicle, 18 November 1871 and 25 April 1872.

Lee, Alfred Emory. *History of the City of Columbus, Capital of Ohio.* Volume 2. New York: Munsell & Co., 1892.

Lewistown Gazette, 2 October 1861.

Levering, John. "Lee's Advance and Retreat at Cheat River." In *Military Essays and Recollections: Papers Read before the Commandery of the State of Illinois, Military Order of the Loyal Legion of the United States.* Volume 4. Chicago: Cozzens & Beaton Company, 1907.

Logue, Larry M. *To Appomattox and Beyond: The Civil War Soldier in War and Peace.* Chicago: Ivan R. Dee, 1996.

McAulay, John D. *Civil War Breech Loading Rifles.* Lincoln, RI: Andrew Mowbray, Inc., 1993.

McCoy, George W. "Roan's Cloudland Hotel Famous in 19th Century." *Asheville Citizen*, 11 June 1950.

McDonough, James Lee. *War in Kentucky: From Shiloh to Perryville.* Knoxville: University of Tennessee Press, 1994.

McEvoy, Henry N. *McEvoy's Shelbyville, Greensburg and Rushville City Directories and Business Mirrors for 1860–61.* Indianapolis: H. N. McEvoy, Publisher and Compiler, 1861.

McGee, B. F. *History of the 72nd Indiana.* Lafayette, IN: S. Vater & Co., 1882.

McManus, Christopher D., Thomas H. Inglis, and Otho James Hicks, eds. *Morning to Midnight in the Saddle: Civil War Letters of a Soldier in Wilder's Lightning Brigade.* Bloomington, IN: Xlibris Corporation, 2012.

McPherson, James M. *Battle Cry of Freedom.* New York: Oxford University Press, 1988.

Maher, Thomas. "Roan Mountain and Gen. John T. Wilder." *Tennessee Conservationist* 61/4 (July–August 1995): 3–6.
Marcot, Roy M. *Spencer Repeating Firearms.* Irvine, CA: Northwood Heritage Press, 1983.
Meyer, David R. "Midwestern Industrialization and the American Manufacturing Belt in the Nineteenth Century." *Journal of Economic Industry* 49/4 (December 1989): 921–37.
Moore, William H. *Company Town: A History of Rockwood and the Roane Iron Company.* Kingston, TN: Roane County Heritage Commission, Inc., 1984.
———. "Preoccupied Paternalism: The Roane Iron Company in her Company Town—Rockwood, Tennessee." *East Tennessee Historical Society's Publications* 39 (1967): 56–70.
Morton, M. B. "Last Surviving Lieutenant General: Visit to the Home of Gen. S. B. Buckner." *Confederate Veteran* 17/2 (February 1909): 83.
Myers, Robert J., and Louis O. Shudde. "Mortality Experience of Union Civil War Veterans." *Transactions of the Society of Actuaries* 7/17 (1955): 63–68.
Mynders, Albert. "Next to the News." *Chattanooga Times,* 1 July 1956, 22.
Michael, W. H. *Official Congressional Directory.* Washington, D.C.: Government Printing Office, 1889.
Noe, Kenneth W. *Perryville: This Grand Havoc of Battle.* Lexington: University Press of Kentucky, 2001.
Poole, Cary Franklin. *A History of Railroading in Western North Carolina.* Johnson City, TN: Overmountain Press, 1995.
Prechtel-Kluskens, Claire. "The Nineteenth-Century Postmaster and His Duties." *NGS NewsMagazine* 33/1 (January/February/March 2007): 35–39. Available at twelvekey.files.wordpress.com/2014/10/ngsmagazine2007-01.pdf.
Roberts, Snyder. "Roane County as Switzerland of America." *Roane County News,* 24 February 1982.
———. "Roane Iron Company Establishes Rockwood after the Civil War." *Roane County News,* 3 February 1982.

———. "Roane Iron Company Expands to Chattanooga." *Roane County News*, 10 February 1982.

———. "Roane Iron is Important to Rockwood's History." *Roane County News*, 27 January 1982.

———. "Rockwood Name Has Rich History." *Roane County News*, 17 March 1982.

———. "Rockwood Streets Named to Honor City Fathers." *Roane County News*, 10 March 1982.

Rogers, T. A. "John T. Wilder: Soldier and Citizen." *Chattanooga Times*, 12 July 1936.

Shaw, Archibald. *A History of Dearborn County*. Indianapolis: B. F. Bowen & Company, 1915.

Shaw, W. L. "Hard Fighting—Franklin—Munfordville." *Confederate Veteran* 17/5 (May 1909): 221–22.

Sheppard, Muriel Earley. *Cabins in the Laurel*. Chapel Hill: University of North Carolina Press, 1991.

Sievers, Harry Joseph. *The Harrison Horror*. Fort Wayne, IN: Public Library of Fort Wayne and Allen County, 1956.

Smith, Timothy. *The Golden Age of Battlefield Preservation*. Knoxville: University of Tennessee Press, 2008.

Somers, Robert. *The Southern States Since the War, 1870–1871*. Tuscaloosa: University of Alabama Press, 1965.

Stahl, Ray. *Greater Johnson City: A Pictorial History*. Norfolk, VA: Donning Company Publishers, 1986.

Stanley, Matthew E. *The Loyal West*. Urbana: University of Illinois Press, 2017.

Stevenson, David A. M. *Indiana's Roll of Honor*. Indianapolis, IN: A. D. Streight, 1866.

Stickles, Arndt M. *Simon Bolivar Buckner*. Chapel Hill: University of North Carolina Press, 1940.

Sunderland, Glenn. *Lightning at Hoover's Gap*. New York: T. Yoselloff, 1969.

Swedberg, Carrie E., ed. *Three Years with the 92nd Illinois: The Civil War Diary of John M. King*. Mechanicsville, PA: Stackpole Books, 1999.

Sykes, E. T. "An Incident of the Battle of Munfordville, Ky. September 14th, 1862." *Publications of the Mississippi Historical Society* 2 (1918): 536–48.

Taylor, William Alexander. *Centennial History of Columbus and Franklin County, Ohio*. Chicago: S. J. Clarke Publishing Co, 1909.

Terrell, W. H. H. *Indiana in the War of the Rebellion*. Indianapolis, IN: Douglass & Conner, 1869.

Thornbrough, Emma Lou. *Indiana in the Civil War Era, 1850–1880*. Indianapolis: Indiana Historical Bureau & Indiana Historical Society, 1965.

Van Noppen, John J. *Western North Carolina since the Civil War*. Boone, NC: Appalachian Consortium Press, 1973.

Waite, John R. *The Blue Ridge Stemwinder*. Johnson City, TN: Overmountain Press, 2003.

The War of the Rebellion: A Compilation of the Official Records of the Union and Confederate Armies. Washington D.C.: Government Printing Office, 1880–1891. Cited as *OR*.

Watterson, Henry. *"Marse Henry": An Autobiography*. Volume 2. New York: George H. Doron Co., 1919.

Way, William, Jr. *The Clinchfield Railroad*. Chapel Hill: University of North Carolina Press, 1931.

Wheeler, Hazel. *The History of Wilder, Davidson, Highland Junction, Sandy, and "The Hollow."* Jamestown, TN: Fentress Courier, 1992.

Wilder, Moses H. *Book of the Wilders*. New York: E. O. Jenkins, 1878.

"Wilder Point for a Home." *Chattanooga Times*, 12 May 1912.

Wiley, Bell Irvin. *The Life of Billy Yank*. Indianapolis: Charter Books, 1962.

Williams, Samuel Cole. *General John T. Wilder*. Bloomington: Indiana University Press, 1936.

———. *History of Johnson City and Its Environs*. Johnson City, TN: Watauga Press, 1940.

Wilson, Jennifer Bauer. *Roan Mountain: A Passage of Time*. Winston-Salem: John F. Blair Publisher, 1991.

Wiltse, Leah Showers. *Pioneer Days in the Catskill High Peaks*. Hensonville, NY: Black Dome Press Corp., 1999.

Winters, William. *The Musick of the Mocking Birds, the Roar of the Cannon: The Civil War Diary and Letters of William Winters.* Lincoln: University of Nebraska Press, 1998.

Woodworth, Steven E. *Nothing But Victory: The Army of the Tennessee, 1861–1865*. New York: Alfred A. Knopf, 2005.

Zinn, Jack. *R.E. Lee's Cheat Mountain Campaign.* Parsons, WV: McClain Printing Company, 1974.

Index